TWENTYFOURSEVEN

WHERE'S THE MONEY RONNIE?

LEFT (SMALLTIME)

TWENTYFOURSEVEN
Paul Fraser and Shane Meadows

WHERE'S THE MONEY RONNIE?
LEFT (SMALLTIME)
Shane Meadows

First published in 1998
by ScreenPress Books

28 Castle Street Eye Suffolk IP23 7AW

Photoset by Parker Typesetting Service, Leicester
Printed in England by Clays Ltd, St Ives plc

A CIP record for this book
is available from the British Library

ISBN 1–901680–07–X

For more information on forthcoming ScreenPress Books,
contact the publishers at:

ScreenPress Books
28 Castle Street
Eye Suffolk
IP23 7AW
or fax on: 01379 870 261

Contents

Bob Hoskins' Acceptance Speech, Berlin Film Awards, 1997

This is wonderful, getting prizes is a great thrill, obviously, but, to be singled out with *TwentyFourSeven* is, well . . .

Let me try to explain what this means to me.

Now, Shane Meadows is this astonishingly young talent from Nottingham, which is a town in the middle of England, and its probably got the highest crime rate in Europe.

By young I mean he's just twenty-four – just, it makes you sick; and, without much support, for the past several years, he and his team of friends have been making films on the streets of Nottingham.

If you have ever seen these films you can see that they are straight from the heart of the street, and when Scala backed Shane to do his first feature film, the fact that he included me on his team, well, obviously, it was an extraordinary honour, but it was probably one of the most terrifying experiences of my life.

I walked into this gang of kids – you know, I thought 'Ahh', here I am, this fossilised old fogie. But they didn't, they didn't see me like that, they just included me, they didn't expect me to lead and didn't ask me to follow.

I was just one of the chaps and, I'll tell you, at my age to realise your street cred is still intact and the chaps still see you as one of them is great.

Thank you very very much.

Bob Hoskins

Introduction

John McVicar and Jimmy Boyle were my heroes as a boy. The idea of a criminal record and getting one over on the screws in prison seemed the only way forward when I was a lad. They weren't just pipedreams, I was going to be 'infamous'. My first crime was the spending of £17 of sponsored walk money on an industry-standard size box of pineapple cubes. My best friend Wayne Barrett and I ate about forty pence worth, were sick, then threw them in the river and lied every day to our teachers about the money's whereabouts until we were the first eleven-year-old kids ever to have grey hair. A bad start got worse. I got caught buying, not stealing, a stolen set of limited edition John Lowe darts. I also admitted to stealing and eating an egg custard from Sainsbury's. I shot my other best friend Paul Fraser in the guts by accident with an air rifle and wasn't allowed near him for three years.

Some thirteen years later at the age of twenty-two a crime took place that humiliated me above all the others; to be honest it ended my criminal career. I stood up in court to have my charge read out and, along with the people in the gallery laughing at me, the judge and all his mob laughed as well. I didn't even get fined the day I stole the breast pump. It was probably on that same day that I became a film-maker.

NOTTINGHAMSHIRE CONSTABULARY

CHARGE SHEET

Charge Sheet No. ....

ACCUSED COPY

SURNAME: MEADOWS (Mr./Mrs./Miss): FIRST NAMES: SHANE Male ADDRESS : 17, JUBILEE STREET SNEINTON, NOTTINGHAM, Date of Birth : 26/12/1972 Age : 22 years	PTI Unique Ref. No. : 31/NN/859/95 Divisional Crime No.: .... Custody Record No. : 1574/95 NN Station : CENTRAL Division : CE
Occupation : U/E	
Juveniles or Mental Illness/Handicap...... School Attended or Attending........	
Full Name of Appropriate Adult: Address:	OFFICER IN CASE Name JANE HAZARD Rank/No. CON 2109 Station CENTRAL Division CE
Telephone:	

You are charged with the offences shown below. You do not have to say anything unless you wish to do so, but what you do say may be given in evidence.

DETAILS OF CHARGE(S) INCLUDING LEGAL AUTHORITY

1   On the 17th day of March 1995   at At Nottingham in the City of Nottingham
    stole a breast pump to the value of £33.00   (Offence Code : LAAK   )
    belonging to Boots the Chemist.

    Contrary to Section 1(1) of the Theft Act 1968.

Officer Accepting Charge:SGT A. M. AINLEY   178   Station:CENTRAL
Date charged:17/03/95   Time charged: ...17.45..........
Signature of person charging: *Jane Hazard*   CON JANE HAZARD 2109

I SHANE MEADOWS of 17, JUBILEE STREET, SNEINTON, NOTTINGHAM,
acknowledge that I must appear at NOTTINGHAM (GUILDHALL) Magistrates Court at 09:30 on
Wednesday the 19/04/95 to answer charges mentioned hereon.

WARNING   YOU HAVE A STATUTORY DUTY TO COMPLY WITH YOUR BAIL AND SURRENDER
       YOURSELF INTO CUSTODY AT THE PLACE AND TIME SHOWN ABOVE. IF YOU
       FAIL TO DO SO YOU MAY BE PROSECUTED AND MAY BE LIABLE TO A FINE OR
       TERM OF IMPRISONMENT NOT EXCEEDING TWELVE MONTHS OR BOTH.

At sixteen years old I couldn't even get a job as a clown's assistant, now look at me, forty-six wives, a Lambourgini, a minor island just off the coast from Papua New Guinea (near Marlon Brando's) and not to forget a career as a film-maker.

Anyone and everyone is capable of making a film. I have no time for moaning bastards who'd rather sit and watch taped episodes of *Kilroy* than do something out of the ordinary. There's no point in complaining that it takes thousands of quid and isn't for the likes of us – I'm twenty-five, I got kicked out of school before my O levels, my mum works in a chippie and my dad drives a lorry. You can do it if you have a bit of talent and you stick at it. You can make a film, no sweat, for £100.

All the other stuff is bullshit. I made my first films for a tenner with money I saved from my dole. What I'd do was buy those five-packs of very dicey noodles for a pound, a couple of cans of pineapple chunks and a jar of peanut butter and I'd live on that for a fortnight. OK, my pineapple and noodle satay wasn't the tastiest thing ever to hit a plate, and it was pretty awful nutritionally, but it allowed me to buy videotape and it got me going. You could say my film career was launched by the DSS.

I borrowed a camcorder from Intermedia Film and Video in Nottingham, who let me muck around in their editing suite and use their equipment in return for working for them for nothing. I was living on a council estate at the time (I still am) and I tried to get my friends to help – they were like me, unemployed, single mothers and that sort of thing, ducking and diving. But they all thought I was mad, and that I didn't want to be in 'Jeremy Beadle movies', so I had to do it on my own: the camera, the acting, the works. I put the camcorder on a tripod and shot myself – it was bonkers and I nearly had it pinched a few times, but I got something on film and started editing it. When I showed it to the people on the street, they thought it was great and they all wanted to be in the next one. There was no stopping me after that. We started doing lots of little ten-minute comedies and serial killer flicks set on the estate. We used to do one a month.

After about a year, we decided to save up to make a short film we could show somewhere. So, with the help of Intermedia, we made one for £200 and tried to get it shown in the local area. But it was no-go, none of the film festivals would take video films, so we set up our own. Twice a month, we held a thing called 'Six of the Best' in an old flea-pit porn-style cinema in Nottingham. You paid 50p to have your film shown to 75 people. Most weeks, there were a lot more than six films there. It has now turned into an international video festival called Flip Side.

Setting that up inspired a lot of people in the area to get off their arses. When they saw that people could make films, they decided to have a go. We set up a thing called 'Film of the Day' – we put an ad in the local paper, brought together a whole load of people and made a film in a day. Heaps of people turned up. We went out with them in the morning and improvised these big crowd scenes. We started off with a *Ben-Hur* chariot race using shopping trollies which then turned into a sort of *Invasion of the Zombies*.

We had all these people wandering into the shops in Nottingham pretending to be zombies and scaring shop assistants. It was great. We finished it with a *Dance of the Zombies* in a pub. At the end of that day, we showed them how to edit it and then we screened it. The response was fantastic because they saw there was no bullshit. And that has carried on. We went on to make *Where's the Money Ronnie?*, which got me work on a documentary for Channel 4, which got me the money for *Smalltime*. It is an hour long and cost us £4,500. Starting out though, you can really do quite a good little ten-minute number for £100. Most video shops hire out camcorders for about £15 a day. Tapes cost £6 each, and they give you an hour and a half's worth of film. Don't worry about running out of tape, keep shooting, you can always get another tape. Another good tip is to beg, borrow or steal a wheelie bin which you can use as a tracking trolley. It may sound zany but it works. You can hire edit suites pretty cheap up here in the Midlands (£15 to £20 a day is about right).

It is actually possible to edit with the camera, I used to do it a lot. As for costumes, I usually allow about £30 for a raid on a Scope charity shop. You can get some really crazy things. But people tend to rise to the occasion anyway with their own zany clothes if you're really strapped. That probably leaves just about enough to get pissed with – which is always the most important part of the budget.

Writing scripts is not as hard as it seems. Stick to things you know and you'll not go wrong. Both *Smalltime* and *Where's the Money Ronnie?* are about the people I grew up with in Uttoxeter. It's as working-class as it gets – full of Irish, Scots, Brummies and Stokies who came to work for JCB in the sixties. My memories of the men I grew up around were of small-time crooks, good people who had been shat on during the recession, trying to get by by skimming a bit off the top. When I was a kid, I wanted to be one of these people who had taken a few knocks but managed to survive without killing anybody by being a bit enterprising. People only steal to have a better life and I remember stuff being shared around among people on the breadline, who would never have been able to afford it unless it was knocked off.

When I started doing filming, I used these characters. I remember this Scottish guy who claimed he had won a lottery, and even went to the papers claiming he was now a millionaire. He then took a copy of the paper into a pub, got them to throw a party for him and invited all his friends. He bought a couple of grands' worth of tropical fish into the bargain. Of course, he was caught and he went down, but he gave everyone a good time in the process. *Where's the Money Ronnie?* and *Smalltime* are full of people like this prepared to do anything within reason for the buzz. I've got so much material from where I grew up and from my parents. They taught me to be proud of what I was and that has stood me in good stead. They didn't hide anything from me as a child, so I was exposed to all these mad characters and stories, and I'm very grateful to them.

Now things are taking off for me, and with *TwentyFourSeven* I've got a deal with Company Pictures to give money back to young film-makers and musicians in my area. There are two brilliant twelve-year-old girls who've made a film in the Midlands. The talent is there. Even though *TwentyFourSeven* cost £1.5 million, I don't think I'm ever going to make a load of cash from films.

I want to make the films I want, and shove the rest if you can't have fun. You will make bad films as well as good ones, so you have to enjoy yourself. I've got a mortgage now but it's for a council house. I'm not about to lose my roots and move to Hollywood. I'm happy where I am.

Shane Meadows

[Elements of this introduction first appeared in the *Guardian*]

For Joseph Chatfield, my family and the people of Uttoxeter

SHANE

For my family from Uttoxeter to Nottingham and the Various Scampis we have had

PAUL

Naishe.

SHANE AND PAUL

In memoriam
Wayne Barrett

TWENTYFOURSEVEN

Paul Fraser and Shane Meadows

TWENTYFOURSEVEN

When I was a young boy hanging around with my lifelong and best friend Paul Fraser there was a man in our town who set up a football club for the town's various ruffians. Initially we all joined for the free fish and chips but then, as the first few drastic losses came in and the press began to dub us the worst football team in history, we began to really feel part of something special. That something has stayed with me my whole life; it's called faith. No matter what happened in and around the football club, and it usually did happen at least four times, and even if we only had prisons left to play in the club's latter stages, our coach Naishe Higges never stopped believing in us. The spirit and belief of men like Naishe inspired myself and Paul to write, celebrate and give dignity to *TwentyFourSeven.*

Shane Meadows

I EXT. DISUSED TRAIN STATION – DAY

This first scene is set in the present. We are introduced to Darcy, a man of about forty. His condition gives him the impression of a battered tramp.

Darcy is lying in an old disused train station – one which he had previously taken great pride in cleaning as a tribute to his love of the town. This shelter has been his Mecca, where he'd come to structure his thoughts and debate, with himself, his theories on life. The images around the shelter will project the nature of Darcy's present condition – that of a man unkept, derelict and on the brink of destruction.

We see Darcy in a wide shot from the opposite side of the station – a stream of piss coming from him, the rugged features of a desert traveller, the wino with Thunderbirds falling from his weakening grasp.

The scene changes to a wide shot of a Man walking along the now disused track leading to the old shelter. He is walking his dog. We see this Man and then the dog – the camera focuses. We hear the occasional instruction.

MAN

Woody, leave it, boy.

Et cetera. We see the Man's foot treading into a poo laid by someone else's hound. The camera tracks backwards to reveal Darcy lying in the shelter as the Man and the dog approach. Woody is then seen tugging and pulling at Darcy's arm which is coming out of the shelter. Without much concern for the figure within, the Man proceeds to clean his shoe on the edge of the shelter.

Leave it, Woody. Woody, ya dirty shit, put it away.

The dog is trying to mount Darcy's arm.

Woody . . .

The Man then pulls the dog away from Darcy. It will soon become apparent that the Man knows Darcy – but at present the incident seems insignificant. As he pulls his dog away he notices blood on and around Darcy's head. We cut to a shot from behind Darcy inside the shelter as the Man bends down to check him out.

You alright there, mate? Hello . . . hello.

The dog has sat down and is cuddled up between Darcy's legs.

Woody, ya daft spazz. Come on . . . off.

The Man makes to leave Woody, who now seems to be guarding Darcy.

Woody . . .!

While he is making a final attempt to retrieve his dog, the penny drops and he recognises Darcy.

Darcy . . . Is that you, mate? Darcy?

On hearing the word 'Darcy' the dog becomes excitable, scurrying in small circles and yelping.

Shut it, Woody. Darcy, mate, you alright?

We begin an edgy hand-held sequence using jump cuts to illustrate the Man taking Darcy from the shelter, loading him into his car.

2 EXT. TIM'S FLAT – DAY

Turning up at the Man's (Tim's) flat and finally taking him to rest in the bedroom.

3 INT. TIM'S FLAT – BEDROOM – DAY

Upon arrival in Tim's bare bedroom – continuing the hand-

held sequence – he strips Darcy of his clothes and places him in the bed. The man has the impression that Darcy is suffering from concussion and excess booze.

Woody jumps onto the bed and curls up at the foot of the bed.

TIM

Ya soft mutt, Woody.

4 INT. TIM'S FLAT – KITCHEN – DAY

In master shot only. In the kitchen, Tim puts all of Darcy's dirty clothes into the machine and waits for it to begin its cycle. In the pocket of Darcy's big overcoat he finds a diary. The kettle whistles on the hob. He pours himself a coffee and we cut to another master shot of him sitting at the table. He makes himself a roll-up, lights it, crosses his legs and leans forward. He pulls the diary close and opens it.

Scraps of paper and loose photos fall out. He gathers them, puts them on the table and begins to read. The camera cuts to an overhead shot of the photos on the table and the title sequence begins.

TITLE SEQUENCE: *a montage of brief scenes charting the life of Alan Darcy from childhood to manhood.*

5 EXT. GARDEN – DAY

This title sequence will consist of a montage of short scenes and still photographs (all overlaid with titles), giving the audience a sense of Alan Darcy's family and history. All shot on Super 8.

As a child: scenes with his Mother and Father in the garden juxtaposed against a series of photos showing them on holiday flying a model aeroplane, etc.

The soundtrack 'Monkey Dead' by Gavin Clarke will run throughout. As the title sequence ends and the music begins to fade, we cut back to Scene 3. The music slightly overlaps and fades to silence.

6 EXT. DISUSED TRAIN STATION – DAY

Five years previous to the first three scenes.

We are in a wide shot looking over the train track onto a tatty platform. We can see Darcy walking along with a broom in his hands, sweeping the floor. The camera remains still throughout this scene. As Darcy continues to sweep and pick up the litter he stops by the shelter and begins to read the graffiti.

>   DARCY
>   (*voice-over*)
> We all die in the beginning, so it's all about living, I suppose. I was a forgotten thirty-something in the eighties; everything was a boom, a transaction, a big take-over. The birth of the computer age and the death of the small-town work force. Money was God, money is God. When our town died, we, with our young in hand, were beginning, but we weren't living. I feel as though I'm a casualty, but that's cool, I suppose, because most of us feel that way.

7 EXT. CHIP SHOP – HIGH ST – DAY

We see a group of Lads standing outside a chip shop with Darcy eating fish and chips. They look as if they have all been jogging as they are sweating and look totally knackered. Darcy is talking to them about his boxing days.

>   DARCY
>   (*putting a whole pickled egg in his mouth*)
> I tell you though, Lads. No bull. You'll have all the girls after you.

>   STUART
> How d'ya work that one out?

DARCY

What about Sylvester Stallone?

BENNY

That was a film though, Darcy.

There is an all-round pause as they eat and ponder . . . Darcy winks, laughs at their baffled faces and leaves.

We see them eating their chips around a bench outside the chip shop.

We cut to a shot of another group of Lads (Knighty, Daz, Gadget and Meggy) walking along the high street towards the chip shop.

We cut back to the Lads eating their chips. They are seen to notice the approaching Group.

We cut back to the Lads, panning around them as they get closer.

We cut back to the Lads eating; they are seen to spit on their chips as the action returns to real time. They are spitting on their chips so that the Nasty Lads approaching will not take their chips.

DAZ

What have you just done?

BENNY

I've spat on them.

DAZ

Have you done it as well?

The other Lads nod.

I can't believe that. Have you spat on the sausages as well?

Benny nods again.

That's dark, that is. I never have your chips, you mardy little arse. First time I ask and ya gob on them.

Daz looks to Knighty, as if to get an opinion. He takes the half-eaten sausage from Benny's bag. He wobbles it in front of Benny then jabs it into his eye. Benny screams because the sausage is hot.

Don't be so insensitive next time.

He grabs the chips from Benny and chucks them at the window of the chippy. The Lads laugh and walk away, leaving Benny with a red eye and the other Lads feeling pretty useless and wank.

8 EXT. 60S HOUSING ESTATE – DAY

Monologue over four shots from around the local housing estate observing the multitude of nicotine-grey buildings, the final shot finishing outside Tim's (the man who found Darcy at the train track).

DARCY
(*voice-over*)
Housing development, housing de-vel-op-ment, of what? Two thousand people in an area where there should be two hundred maximum. Development's a cagey word, it's like 'fresh frozen'. Twelve square feet of turf, a different colour door to the neighbour, maybe a tiled front if you know someone in the trade.

From outside Tim's house we cut to three shots inside to reveal:

9 INT. TIM'S HOUSE – FRONT ROOM – DAY

Tim's alcoholic Father asleep on the sofa.

Tim's overweight Mum ironing in the kitchen and . . .

11 INT. TIM'S HOUSE — BEDROOM — DAY

Tim in his box room reading Judge Dredd.

> DARCY
> (*voice-over*)
> Other than that you get four walls of bricks, furniture
> that cries out second-hand and poor, and the
> demoralised inhabitants who've lost touch with their
> origins. Behind these walls are people. Tim lives with his
> family in one of these houses. The guy is getting shit
> twenty-four: seven, the problem is he thinks there's
> nothin' he can do about it.

*The camera is still on Tim, sitting in his room reading his
comic. Woody is sitting on his bed with him. Loud banging is
heard from the stairs. We cut to hand-held for the rest of the
scene as Tim's door bursts open and his Dad storms in. The
dog growls and leaves. Tim's Dad is very drunk, slurring his
words, spitting, etc.*

> GEOFF THE DAD
> You're fuckin' useless. I asked you to get your mother's
> fags twenty years ago, and what do you do ah? What do
> you do ah . . .? Ah . . .? Am fuckin' talkin' to ya right?
> So put the fuckin' shit down now, we should have put
> you in a home years ago but ya mother said no, no we
> can't, she says. But ya know what ah tit face, ya know
> what she's sayin' now, don't ya . . .? Yer, that's right, she
> wants ya fuckin' out. Too fuckin' late now I tells the fat
> cow, too fuckin' late now.

Geoff walks out and then walks back in.

Where's me fuckin' toothbrush?!

As he re-enters the room he trips on the carpet and lands face down on the floor. As this happens there is a knock at the door, Tim gets up and climbs over his Dad who continues to shout as Tim leaves the room.

Two fucking quid that toothbrush cost me, and where's all my Strepsils? Someone sat by the side of my bed and sucked all me fucking Strepsils.

12 EXT. LOCAL PARK – DAY

A group of five Lads are sat under a big tree smoking spliffs and drinking cans of Kwik Save beer. One of the Lads, Tim, has bruising around his face. There is rope swinging from a branch where the Lads have been playing. One is resting on a football. They are doing what they do every day – get battered, joke around and stir up trouble. Although there is the odd cutaway we stay mainly in wide shot.

KNIGHTY

It's a bee. It's a friggin' bee. Look, it's got a fing on its arse.

GADGET

Bees don't have things on their arses.

KNIGHTY

Yes, they do, where d'ya think the sting comes from, their bank card?

DAZ

Shit, I haven't signed on yet . . . What time is it?

GADGET

No, no. Bees bite and wasps sting, there's one of them poems so you can remember, like. You know that thing, April, June, September, November? It's like that like but it's about bees and wasps.

(passing a spliff)

D'ya want this?

The Lads feel really sorry for Tim; there is a pause.

It's four o'clock by the way, Daz.

DAZ

Oh shit, I missed it yesterday as well.

MEGGY

Which are the ones that die after they've stung ya?

GADGET

Bees, innit? 'Cause they're the workers, like. They do all
the grafting for the Queen, getting' her shit together an
that. An if they get any hassle then . . .

GADGET

. . . they shoot their load into someone's arm and die, it's
a real nightmare if you think about it.

KNIGHTY

Shut up, ya fool.

DAZ

Listen, can someone sub us? My Giro won't be here till
Christmas an' I've ordered some whizz off Fagash, if I
don't pick it up he'll break my legs.

MEGGY

I'll lend you twenty if you lend us your Honda Melody
tonight.

DAZ

If you give us twenty, you can borrow my Honda
Melody Classic Express Turbo Maximus Beast.

MEGGY

I'll give you twenty and then you'll only owe me ten.

DAZ

Go on, then.

MEGGY

No, I don't want to now.

Everyone bursts out laughing.

In the distance we see and hear Darcy driving up towards the Lads in a Reliant Robin. He's wearing a piss-pot helmet and listening to his on-board DIY stereo system, which is a Walkman attached to a big old speaker.

They can't help but spot him and their attention/conversation turns to him. He takes off his helmet, takes a comb from his pocket and brushes the sides of his hair. He turns the music up and proceeds to waltz over to the group . . .

KNIGHTY

Here comes Lieutenant Darcy Fruitcake the Fifth.

MEGGY

He's off his head, man. I saw him on a stepladder in the middle of town. He just stood there watching everyone.

KNIGHTY

He used to hang around with my old man when they were in the boxing club.

To Darcy, who is still waltzing over to them.

What are you doing down here?

DARCY

It's me, boys. Hard at work again? Am practising me moves for the ladies.

KNIGHTY

Is this the geriatric society, Darcy?

DARCY

Not far off the mark there, Ian.

Am I not? Shall I keep guessing?

DARCY
Mmm . . . no, you'll only bore me.

Darcy is rubbing his tash, demonstrating its ability to help him think.

KNIGHTY
You look a right divvy, Darcy. He's lost it, Lads.

DARCY
I haven't lost it at all, Ian, I'm quite secure in what I'm about, young man. I've got plans and I've got direction.

KNIGHTY
(*lost for something to say*)
You've got something stuck under your nose, mate.

A couple of the Lads laugh.

DARCY
Do you think it's strange? . . . As it happens I grew this moustache for people like you, it's probably the first time today any of you've thought with your brain and not your arses.

KNIGHTY
(*getting defensive*)
What do you do, Darcy?

DARCY
I'll tell you what I don't do. Sausages, red eyes and greasy chip shop windows.

DAZ
You've heard of Bird's-Eye, well that was Benny's eye.

Nobody laughs except Darcy.

DARCY

I like that, Darren. Have you thought about being a sit-down comedian before?

DAZ

Eh?

DARCY

Ronnie Corbett is looking for a YTS, maybe I could help you write a letter . . .

All the Lads have been well and truly baffled and are lost for words. Darcy cracks a very knowing smile.

Anyway, Lads, I must go and have dinner with a beautiful lady. Take care not to wet your beds. Bye.

Darcy jogs off towards his Reliant Robin. There is a slight pause.

DAZ

Was he being serious about that comedian thing?

As Darcy drives off into the distance the Lads carry on muttering among themselves. We stay with the Lads as Darcy's voice-over begins. As the voice-over continues, we see the Lads get up and play football, this remains in a wide shot.

DARCY
(*voice-over*)

Reputations are so important in a town like this. If your father was a big man, then you get given an aura of invincibility. Some think that you're going to be as hard as he was, others are just scared that the dad will dust you if you dust their son. Knighty's like that.

13 INT. PUB – DAY

Cut to a shot of Knighty with his Dad sitting in a pub.

DARCY
(*voice-over*)

His dad is a saint, he was a hard man in his day but he's older and wiser now. Daz's dad was hard in his day too, but he still lives off it, 'cause he's got nowhere – he's a bigger idiot than his son.

14 EXT. STREET – DAY

Cut to shot of Daz and his Dad walking down the street together. Daz's Dad is animating one of his old boxing yarns.

DARCY'S
(*voice-over*)

That's why Daz is always 'The Lads, the Lads this and the Lads that.'

15 EXT. LOCAL PARK – DAY

Back to the Lads playing football. We hear the sound of 'Fruit Tree' by Nick Drake fading in as the voice-over finishes.

DARCY
(*voice-over*)

None of them is singularly strong enough to break away and say, wait a minute . . . there must be more than this. No one, that's why nothing ever changes.

16 INT. DARCY HOUSE – BATHROOM – DAY

The music from the previous sequence runs through into this sequence.

We are now in Darcy's bathroom as he shaves. Four short hand-held tracking shots observe Darcy as he shaves and puts on his dancing shoes, etc., in the bathroom.

As the music continues we see:

17 EXT. STREET – DAY

A shot of Darcy riding his motorcycle with his Aunty Iris in the sidecar; we see them ride past and the camera pans to follow them.

18 EXT. COMMUNITY CENTRE – DAY

They pull up outside a community centre. The music continues as soundtrack.

19 INT. COMMUNITY CENTRE HALL – DAY

Inside the hall as Darcy and Aunty Iris enter and, as the camera tracks backwards, we see a choreographed sequence take place, with about four other Couples dancing in the hall. This is all one shot. The camera tracks backwards down the hall as the music continues, the two of them shining out among the others as they light up the hall. As the music begins to fade we cut to the next scene.

20 INT. BOXING CLUB/GYM – DAY

The room is empty. The camera (Jimmy Jib) begins in the ring then glides gently backwards over the top rope towards the back of the room.

We see the old posters and bits and pieces of equipment as we move further back.

We hear two voices from outside and a door to the room opening. At this point the camera turns quite sharply towards the door and we see Darcy with the Lads (Stuart, Youngy and Benny) standing in the doorway. As the voice-over begins we cut to:

21 INT. BOXING CLUB – CHANGING ROOM – DAY

A wide shot in the changing room with the Lads.

DARCY
(*voice-over*)
Knighty and co. resent this lot because they've had a
better start in life than themselves; they have always been
told they are the gutter. At the end of the day it doesn't
matter how much or how little you have. If you have
never had anything to believe in, you're always going to
be poor.

*Darcy walks past them and into the toilet dressed in his
dancing suit with matching white pumps.*

Benny and the Lads have agreed to try and make this
boxing club work, that's all the commitment I need from
them. I just wish it was that simple to get through to
Knighty; I'd love to bring the two ends of town together
like the boxing club we had as kids. In the ring, when
you catch one on the nose it doesn't hurt any less
because your house is posher than the other guy's.

22 INT. BOXING CLUB – DAY

*Towards the end of the monologue we cut to a shot of the
Lads sitting in a small group in the ring. Darcy returns from
the toilets in a tight-fitting white and grey tracksuit, with a
large pair of leather boots. No one bats an eyelid. We cut into
conversation.*

DARCY
How'd ya feel about me bringing a few people over
that'll have some proper spars with ya?

YOUNGY
You've got to be joking, Darcy. I'm doing it for the
fitness, you know, a bit of fun.

DARCY
Sparring isn't boxing, Lads, it's an art form. You just
take it easy so you can pick up the skills.

18

STUART

We aren't trying to be boxers, Darcy.

BENNY

Don't trust him, Lads, I can smell a rat, and it can't be in my pants 'cause I've just put them on.

DARCY

(*sarcastic but humorous*)
It can't be me either, I don't wear pants.

They all laugh.

STUART

Who've you got in mind for this sparring then?

DARCY

Knighty and co.

Everything goes silent and we hear the sound of the wind whistling through the trees.

If they're picking on you, then maybe you can teach them a thing or two in the ring . . . What? Why?

The Lads are clearly not into that idea one iota. We quickly cut to a shot of each Lad as he gives a quicksure answer.

Benny points at his burnt eye.

BENNY

Hot!

YOUNGY

Ooh, me neck.

He gestures pain.

STUART

Chance, no and frigging spring to mind.

YOUNGY

Ooh, me back.

Pain gesture.

DARCY

What you scared of?

STUART

What do you think?

23 EXT. FIELDS — DAY

We see Knighty, Fagash, Daz, Tim, Meggy and Gadget walking along an old beaten track in the country. They all have tracksuits and wellingtons on. The camera is still and observes them as they all walk past. Knighty has an air pistol, the rest have catapults, except for Gadget who is holding a sword. No one has caught anything and as they trudge past they look as if they've been at it for hours. Gadget stops and doubles up in pain. The Lads turn round.

KNIGHTY

What is it, Gadget?

GADGET
(*in severe pain*)

I need a crap.

Everyone bursts out laughing. Fagash pulls out some toilet paper.

FAGASH

I'll sell you some of this.

They all laugh again. That is, except for Gadget, who hits the deck in a bout of pain.

GADGET

Don't be tight, man. Ow! Please, man, this is killing me.

The Lads are wetting themselves.

I had a curry roll from the chippy last night. It's . . .

Ow! Aghh! Come on, Fags, giz it us, mate, please.

Fagash jumps up in the air and throws the toilet paper into the tree.

> FAGASH
> If you can get to it before you poo your pants you can have it for free.

Fagash and the Lads walk off laughing and leave Gadget to his doom. Gadget turns around and runs the other way, half bent over and in pain. We cut to an hour later. The Lads are sitting down in a field. Gadget is nowhere to be seen. Fagash is smoking a spliff. They look cold and pissed off.

> TIM
> We ain't gonna catch anythin', are we?

> DAZ
> We should have gone an' bombed the river, this was a rubbish idea.

> FAGASH
> That's Gadget for you, man.

> KNIGHTY
> Five pound a rabbit, my arse.

Off camera we hear Gadget shouting. The Lads turn around and we see Gadget running towards them holding a rabbit.

> GADGET
> I've got one, Lads.

The Lads looked shocked.

> I told you, didn't I?

Gadget arrives and shows the Lads the rabbit.

> Look at that little beauty.

I don't believe it. You didn't kill that, it's been dead about a month.

The Lads laugh a bit more.

GADGET

So what?!

FAGASH

What did you do, shit down a warren and they sent you that up as a peace offering?

Everyone laughs, including Gadget.

GADGET

It's a start though, Lads, innit?

DAZ

Wrong, man, it's a finish. I'm goin' home.

Daz begins to walk off; the others grab their stuff and follow.

MEGGY

What did you wipe yourself with, Gadget?

GADGET

Me pants and socks.

They all walk off laughing.

24 INT. BOXING CLUB – DAY

We can see Darcy in the boxing club. Throughout the voice-over we see him begin to revamp the space, opening boxes, cleaning equipment and painting walls. This will run as three or four wide shots.

DARCY
(*voice-over*)
This morning is a gift, every morning you have another chance, sometimes you do nothing, sometimes you get

lucky and the day shines on you. But how often do you wake up and seize the day with your own hands, make that day your own? The Lads and the people of this town have been living in the same day their whole life. This morning, my friends, is the morning I remove my life from the hands and the strings of fools and try to build a dream, the 101 Boxing Club.

As the voice-over reaches a conclusion, Darcy steps away from his painting and looks around the space, then continues to work. We stay with him for a few seconds. He stands back, admires his work then proceeds again.

25 EXT. FOOTBALL FIELD – DAY

The Lads are playing football, drinking and getting stoned . . . again. Visually this runs very much as the previous park scene.

> KNIGHTY
> It's Darcy, Lads. Daz, ask him about the comedy thing.

Laughter.

> DARCY
> Hello there, Lads, training for the TA again, are we? You know you'll not get in unless you eat a hedgehog, don't you?

> KNIGHTY
> Good one, Darcy.

> DARCY
> I was quite pleased with that one myself, Ian. Giz the ball and I'll show you my silky skills.

The ball is kicked very hard at Darcy; it hits him in the groin.

> Ooww.

The Lads burst into fits of laughter.

You can laugh, Lads, but I still managed to control.
Darren, on your head.

He chips a perfect ball, Daz jumps to header it. The ball hits him in the face and he falls over – the Lads are crying with laughter.

You need to keep your eye on the ball at all times, Darren.

KNIGHTY
I'd hit him for doing that, Daz.

DARCY
Would you now, Ian? Right, Kevin, kick us the ball back again, son. Do you want to come and stand over here, Ian, and I'll hit the ball straight into your face.

KNIGHTY
It's a joke for fuck's sake, Darcy.

DARCY
Oh humour, now that's a fine thing said at the right place and in the right circumstances, Ian. I've got a joke for you boys. What's this?

Darcy makes a circle with his thumb and forefinger, he waves his hand around in the air shouting 'Grrr grrr'.

It's a vicious circle, Lads.

TIM
Darcy you're tapped, mate.

DARCY
If anyone around here is tapped then it's you lot. You're the joke of the town, boys. People may think I'm a bit doolally but they know I'm harmless. But you lot, you intimidate people, don't you? 'Cause you believe that's the key to respect.

Who do you think you are, ah? Any more twisted shit
and I'll knock you out, alright?

Darcy walks over to him and stands face to face with him.

DARCY
No it's not alright, young man. Just think about it,
intimidation, respect, you've got no respect from me
whatsoever, Ian. Now listen, I'm here for a reason, Lads.
I was thinking about you all this morning. I want you to
get involved in a boxing club I'm organising.

KNIGHTY
What do you know about boxing?

DARCY
A hell of a lot more than any of you lot. I used to box
with your dad, Ian, and yours, Darren.

KNIGHTY
Yer I know that, mate, that's why I can fight, it's in my
blood. I'm a natural, like a gypsy.

DARCY
You can't bloody fight, you fool. It's about control, not
hitting someone with anything you can lay your hands
on.

KNIGHTY
You ain't never seen me fight, how do you know if I can
fight or not?

DARCY
Come here, Ian.

*Knighty looks confused and uneasy, but approaches Darcy to
prove he isn't scared.*

Smack me in the mouth.

You'll hit me back.

DARCY

No, I won't, just give us your best.

KNIGHTY

You're not gonna hit me back though?

DARCY

No.

Knighty pulls back his arm and swings, Darcy ducks left, Knighty misses, Darcy follows through by pushing him over.

Lesson one, balance. You're completely off balance, son. An eight year old with a bit of training would have taken you out there. You need to learn the discipline of the sport. It's nothing to do with attacking the opponent until they drop, it's about the whole self, mentally conditioning yourself to pick and plot the course of your fight.

Darcy offers his hand to Knighty, he accepts and is pulled up.

Right how about this, I'll take you on at your sport right now. I'll give you five penalties. If you score three I'll walk away and leave you to your misery but if you don't then you can all come down and give it a go next Tuesday.

KNIGHTY

That's not fair. If we win you leave, if you win we join a boxing club.

DARCY

Fair enough. How about I do a dance in my pants and vest in too?

TIM

Can't ask for more than that, can we?

I'm up for that, Darcy. Lads? It'd be worth it just to see your fat arse move.

The Lads agree. The ball is placed on the penalty spot, Darcy removes his top and walks to the goal. While doing this Knighty hits the ball and scores.

KNIGHTY

That's one out of one.

DARCY

Well that's hardly fair, lads, but good initiative, I'll accept that. Who's next?

The ball is again placed on the spot, Meggy steps up, kicks and scores. The Lads cheer and chant, celebrating as if at Wembley.

Just getting my eye in, boys. Who's next?

Again the ball is placed.

Just the one more then, lads.

Gadget shoots and hits the bar.

Two out of three, lads.

Daz steps up, hits the ball which goes about twenty foot over the bar.

This is it then, back to you, are we, Ian? Right, when you're ready.

Darcy is bouncing around all over the goal, Knighty walks away about a hundred yards then turns and comes sprinting at the ball. He shoots, the ball hits Darcy straight in the groin, which is still sore from earlier.

DARCY

Ahh . . .

Darcy slowly and painfully gets to his feet. He's gasping for breath and is in quite a bit of pain. He picks up his shirt and begins to leave.

Right, I'll see you all on Tuesday. Ouch.

He half jogs and half limps away. The Lads just stand around, quite unaffected.

26 INT. FAGASH'S HOUSE – FRONT ROOM – DAY

We are in Fagash's house. He is sitting in his front room with the Lads and a couple of Girls.

There is a lot of cut-up dope and speed on the table.

In the centre of the room on a table, Knighty is sitting on a chair holding a chess board, a Nintendo and a picture of Elvis.

Daz and Gadget are on the sofa. They have a Crossfire game and an ironing board resting across their legs.

The Girls are holding various household goods: Hoover, iron, etc.

Fagash is sitting down counting a lot of cash. He has sold these things to them. Tomorrow is the day he is to be sent to prison.

> FAGASH
> Well, it would be better for me if I could sell it all in one go.

> KNIGHTY
> We ain't dealers, Fagash. If you split it you'll get more for it anyway.

> FAGASH
> I know. I just want some time by myself, know what I mean?

> DAZ
> Safe, man. Why don't we sell it for you, then bring you the cash?

FAGASH

You've gotta be joking, man. I'd never see you again.

DAZ

Course you will.

FAGASH

Shut the fuck up, Daz. I want cash for it or you can all fuck off.

GADGET

Sorry, man, it was just an idea. We'll buy what we can.

Meggy walks into the front room and see's that everyone has bought everything. He looks pissed off.

MEGGY

You said you weren't starting till three. What a nightmare, is there anything left?

KNIGHTY

Sorry, Meggy, I knew you'd want the Nintendo. So I moved it all forward an hour.

MEGGY

Fuckers.

FAGASH

Right sit down, man. I want to sell the dope and then you can all fuck off an' give me some peace.

Fagash is starting to get tense. The Lads begin to get their money out. Daz's missus gives him the evil eye.

DAZ

What . . .?

POB (DAZ'S MISSUS)

Don't even think about buying any of that with my money.

DAZ

Shut up, will you? I'll spend it on what I like.

No one is bothered by this little argument. They start to buy the dope off Fagash as it continues.

POB

Just see what happens if you do.

DAZ

You bought that Hoover.

POB

And you bought Crossfire.

DAZ

Yeah but you wanted Crossfire as well.

POB

But I did say that was all you could spend. 'Cause you didn't sign on yet, did you? So it's your fault.

DAZ

But the Crossfire was an 'us' thing. An the Hoover was a 'you' thing. So I haven't had a 'me' thing yet. And dope is an 'us' thing as well.

POB

You're not havin' any money.

DAZ

Fagash give us a lay-on.

FAGASH
(putting his scales away)

None left now, Daz.

DAZ

Now look what you've done.

GADGET

I'll sell you some. Twenty an eighth though.

Everyone laughs. There is a knock at the door.

> FAGASH
>
> Meggy, go an tell them to fuck off, and you lot fuck off as well. I don't mean to be nasty, like, but fuck off.

27 INT. TIM'S HOUSE – KITCHEN – DAY

Tim is talking with his mother (Pat). They are sitting in the kitchen of their home. Food is cooking on the stove. Pat is having a fag break in between house 'duties'. Woody is hanging loose around the kitchen. Up until the point when Geoff enters, the camera remains still in simple wide shot. Upon Geoff's entrance we revert to hand-held.

> PAT
>
> Well, if it keeps you out of trouble.

> TIM
>
> I don't get into trouble.

> PAT
>
> Hanging around with them lot you will. You should come to church.

Tim pretends he didn't hear.

> TIM
>
> They're harmless really.

> PAT
>
> And so's your father.

We hear the front door slam. Geoff enters the kitchen. Woody leaves.

> GEOFF
>
> Very fuckin' cozy. I hope you've not forgotten tea tonight.

PAT

It'll be five minutes.

GEOFF

Amazing, fifteen years I've been coming home an' get a
fuckin' cob from the pub . . . you still can't time it right.

He goes to leave.

TIM

Dad . . .

GEOFF

I haven't got any money.

TIM

I don't want any.

GEOFF

What's the problem then?

TIM

I was just talking to mum about joining this boxing club
that Darcy's set up.

GEOFF

You boxing? You didn't last five minutes last time. You'll
give up as soon as you realise how much it hurts.

TIM

It's about training and fitness.

GEOFF

. . . don't come an try an' tell me what boxin's about.

TIM

I wasn't.

GEOFF

Yes you fuckin' was, and don't answer me back.

                    PAT
    Maybe he's doing this for you.

                    GEOFF
    What?

                    PAT
    Boxin's what you did. Maybe he's tryin' to find some
    connection.

                    TIM
    Mum.

                    GEOFF
    Arrh that's nice. OK lets make a connection. Let's box
    now.

*Geoff puts his bag down and his hands up. Tim looks to the
floor.*

    Come on, Wocky.

Tim doesn't respond.

    You're yellow.

He leaves.

28 EXT. BENNY'S HOUSE – DAY

*From across the road we see Stuart and Youngy pulling up
outside Benny's house. A horn beeps and Benny comes out of
his house. He gets in the car and they drive off.*

29 INT. FAGASH'S FLAT – FRONT ROOM – DAY

*With one simple wide shot the camera observes Fagash sitting
in his dingy flat. There is little decor left and all that remains
is mess, mainly comprising takeaway cartons, fag packets,
Rizlas and empty booze cans. There is a dirty blanket over
the window keeping out any strong daylight.*

Furniture consists of a couple of armchairs, a coffee table and a portable television on top of a beer crate. A dingy hole indeed!

Fagash is wearing a suit. (Music: 'Yummy yummy yummy'.) The suit doesn't fit and doesn't go well with his white trainers.

He is smoking a fag that is getting in his eyes while he chops some speed. He then snorts the speed through a biro, which causes him problems when trying to remove the pen. We cut in close to Fagash as he takes his drugs.

He immediately takes a lighter and smokes a bong, inhaling for about half a minute. He sips some beer then pops a pill. He then leans back on his armchair.

FAGASH

Wow . . .

The telephone rings. He ignores it. The door bell rings, he ignores that too. Then follows a more persistent banging of his letter box.

No!

The banging stops, there is a pause then the lounge door opens, it is Darcy. He has a bottle of Lucozade Sport.

DARCY

Hello there, Fagash, I heard the television on, thought you'd be sleeping.

He walks in and sits on the chair opposite Fagash.

FAGASH

The telly's broke.

DARCY

Oh is it? Right. It must have been next door then.

FAGASH

Next door moved away two months ago.

Did they really? Well I must be hungry then? How do you fancy joining me and a few of the Lads in a bit of boxing?

FAGASH
(*completely off his tits*)

Who?

DARCY

Erm, Knighty, Daz, Meggy, Tim, er, Gadget, loads of us, loads of us. I've heard the Lads are pretty fond of you so I thought you could come along, like the booster, man, get them all enthused.

FAGASH

They're fond of me dope and me generous lay-ons, Darcy.

DARCY

Oh, are they?

FAGASH

Yep, dope and lay-ons, mate.

He is becoming more slurred, he still hasn't looked at Darcy.

DARCY

That's a nice suit . . .

Pause, Darcy is contemplating why he bothered.

So are you interested then, Fagash? Tuesday is our first meeting, down the old 101 Club. Fagash?

FAGASH

Hello, Darcy.

DARCY

You're in a bit of a mess, aren't ya . . .? Come down and do some boxing, ah, Fags?

FAGASH

I'd love to, Darcy . . .

DARCY

Oh great . . .

FAGASH

But I can't am in er, am, in er . . . court, am in court and am gettin' sent down. My head's all over the place. A've got to be there in about an hour, I was just finishing all me supplies.

DARCY

I'll come down with you, Fagash, you never know, I could give you a hand, I know how you handle these judges and that.

FAGASH

You'd do that Darcy?

DARCY

Course I will. Let's just get you cleaned up a bit first though.

FAGASH

You're sound, you are, Darcy. All the Lads think you're a weird un, like, but I think you're sound, mate, really sound like.

DARCY

Arr, that's really nice of you, Fagash.

30 EXT. WOOLATON HALL STATELY HOME – DAY

Benny, Youngy and Stuart are sitting outside Woolaton Hall drinking coffee at a table in the morning sunshine.

STUART

So what's her name?

BENNY

Phil.

STUART

And she stopped the night, did she?

BENNY

Yer.

Stuart and Youngy raise their eyebrows and smile.

What . . . Get lost. It was nice, we just cuddled and that, I'm a gentleman.

YOUNGY

Did you tell her you did boxing?

Both he and Stuart have ridiculous smiles on their faces.

BENNY

What's that mean?

YOUNGY

I just wondered how you played it. Was you all nice or mysterious?

STUART

Was you a mumbling arty type?

Both are smiling away.

BENNY

You're just jealous 'cause you can't cope with the thought of losing your nicest friend.

YOUNGY

It's true, we love you so much and the way you challenge our otherwise meaningless existence.

He hugs him.

STUART

Did you tell her you was a boxer then?

                    BENNY
It came up.

                    STUART
Yeeaa . . . He played the hard man with a soft edge.

                    BENNY
I didn't play anything. She's really nice. It was all
straight-talkin', I felt very relaxed.

                    YOUNGY
How relaxed?

                    BENNY
Shut up . . . You can talk Mister Nil, no pwan, none,
never had any relationships.

They all laugh.

31 INT. COURTROOM – DAY

*At a table sit three Judges, two whom Darcy knows. Facing
them is another longer table with Darcy and Fagash on one
side and a stern-looking Prosecutor on the other side. The
Prosecutor is standing delivering the end of his speech, Darcy
is sitting making notes, Fagash is studying a bogey from his
nose.*

                    PROSECUTOR
. . . so it is clear that Mr Fraser had has ample
opportunity to rectify his wayward manner. A
considerable degree of effort and money has been spent
on rehabilitation. His social worker does not even know
him. It is clear that we must give back to the community.
The community deserves a break from Mr Fraser's
narcotic activities.

There's a slight pause before Darcy stands.

DARCY

Hello, Sally, how's Tom?

SALLY THE JUDGE
(*slightly taken aback*)
Fine, thank you. Could you please remember where you are though, Mr Darcy, and stick to matters in hand.

DARCY

Yes, of course, Sally.

Fagash is seen to put his head in his hands. Darcy is holding some paper; it is clear he has just written the following statement.

I know that Wesley has had ample opportunities to try and sort himself out. Like the man over there is saying.

He looks at the Prosecutor.

But every time he has left this court he's just gone back to the same situation; we don't need to fill our prisons up with criminals whose only crime is the degradation of their own lives; he'll be given respect for going down by the mates in his circle.

He puts the piece of paper down.

Look, I've set up a boxing club to get Wesley and his mates doing something. I went to see him this morning to ask him to help me run it. Give him one more chance and I bet the number of young men you get through these doors will go down. Listen, off the record, you were around when the boxing club ran when we were kids. You know yourself what happened. The crime rate went down. We had something to believe in. These Lads are all fighters, survivors. Let them fight within a ring. Give them, give Fagash just one more chance. That's all I've got to say.

32 INT. COURTROOM – DAY

Still shot of outside the building. The camera tracks in towards the door. After a moment Darcy and Fagash walk out of the building. They pause at the entrance.

Removing his tie and messing his hair, Fagash seems very confused to be free.

> FAGASH
>
> Cheers, Darcy. I ain't got a clue what you were on about but sound, mate, sound.

> DARCY
> (*departing*)
> It's no problem, Wesley, just think though before you carry on. Right, I'll see you Tuesday.

> FAGASH
>
> Yer Tuesday, sound.

They shake hands and walk off the camera in separate directions.

33 EXT. WOOLATON HALL GROUNDS – DAY

We see the three Lads strolling through the gardens of the hall. They are seen to be walking along a path, towards the camera.

> YOUNGY
>
> I'm just not into gettin' involved with them too much.

> BENNY
>
> Daz would have loved me to have had a go when we were havin' the chips. I'd have beat him and then got knocked out by Knighty.

> YOUNGY
>
> It's better to just take it.

BENNY

They'll get bored soon enough.

They stroll along in silence for a short while. Benny tries to trip Stuart, he stumbles then recovers. He tries a return trip but Benny sees it coming and jumps, meanwhile Youngy gets involved by tripping Stuart, who does a spectacular tumble and recovery. They're laughing.

34 INT. GADGET'S HOUSE – ATTIC – DAY

Gadget and his Dad are upstairs in the attic. Gadget's Dad is looking for his old boxing boots for Gadget to wear. His Dad is in a reminiscent mood and is showing an interest in and giving a much needed bout of attention to Gadget's new venture.

GADGET'S DAD

I'll show you some of me old moves, son. I had the quickest knockout out of all our lot. I could turn off the light and get into bed before it went dark. You see what you do.

He gets up.

You bend your knees real low and uppercut as you straighten your legs up. The extra power you get is incredible. Another one is . . . Stand up, I need you for this one.

GADGET

Don't hit me.

GADGET'S DAD

Shut up and stand here.

Gadget gets up.

What you do is . . .

Gadget's Dad punches him in the guts by accident. He drops to the floor.

Ooh, shit, sorry, son.

35 INT. THE OASIS BOXING CLUB – DAY

We find ourselves high up in the boxing club looking down on the ring, where Darcy is standing.

TITLE: 2 WEEKS LATER.

The camera is rotating as it falls gently down towards Darcy (Jimmy Jib).

We hear a very powerfully uplifting piece of music. The ambiance demonstrates that the building is Darcy's church.

The camera looks down at the ring and surrounding area, slowly it moves towards the ring. Darcy is standing in the centre. When we reach a few feet away from Darcy's head, the camera arcs around – as if travelling from 12 to 3 on a clock. The camera comes to rest looking at Darcy through the ropes.

As the music continues, there is a short series of close-up shots around the building. They show the new equipment that Darcy has bought – gloves, bags, sponges and buckets, et cetera. Benny, Stuart and Youngy use the other pieces of equipment in the other hand-held shots. The music comes to a dramatic end; at this point the scene changes. The end bar of music is echoed by loud gasps from Tim who is punching pads held up by Darcy in the centre of the ring.

TIM

Argh, argh.

DARCY

Left, left, left. Upper cut, right, right left. Jab, jab, jab, jab . . .

The door to the hall opens and in walks Fagash, smoking a big fat spliff.

FAGASH
(*with a big grin on his face*)
Yeeaaa . . . wicked, alright, Lads.

Strolls over to the ring.

Lookin' good there, mate. Listen cheers for the other
day, big man. A've been on a non-stop piss-up since
Thursday. A really thought a was goin' down. Has he
told you what he did, Quim? Fuckin' wicked he was.

Darcy and Tim have stopped.

*Darcy removes the pads from his hand, goes to the ropes,
climbs through and jumps down. He picks up a bucket of
water and throws it all over Fagash. Fagash begins to curse at
Darcy – what the fuck, et cetera.*

DARCY
That's not the start I wanted to see from you, Wesley.
You could have been in prison now if I didn't call round
to your house. I don't want any of your bloody wacky
baccy inside this place, is that clear?

FAGASH
There was shit-loads in that spliff.

DARCY
I want you to go home, I want you to go home and
think, then come back later. I spoke to Sally the judge
yesterday evening, her and Tom are going to come to
our first tournament and I want you in the ring for that.

*The Lads present look concerned but continue to practise on
the pads. After a short while the rest of the Lads enter: Daz,
Knighty, Gadget and Meggy.*

DAZ
(*dropping an empty beer can into a bin by the door*)
There isn't any more buckets of water about is there,
Darcy?

45

The Lads laugh.

(again he and Tim have stopped)
Get yourselves some shorts and vests from that bag and
get changed, lads, you're late already.

*The scene moves forward to the Lads half walking and half
jogging around the hall. Darcy is at the front; he is fully
committed to this warm-up – bend to the left to touch the
floor, then to the right, star-jumps into the air. The Lads are
not making the effort unless Darcy can see them. They are all
trying to skip, then having the medicine ball dropped onto
their stomach.*

*The main effect of this scene is that the Lads are crap, all they
want to do is get into the ring and box. The warm-ups
continue until we get to the point where they are all in the
ring wearing gloves and head guards. The camera circles
them.*

This is the space, lads. When you step through that rope
you must master control. The animal instincts of boxing
should be controlled by your knowledge. Right, I want
you to stand in a line. Everyone take one of these bull
clips and tie your leg to the person next to you.

The Lads do this.

Right, now I want you to jab then follow through with
your opposite leg. Keep doing this till you get to the
other side.

*This exercise is a failure. Darcy continues by showing the Lads
a few simple combinations before putting them in pairs to
fight. Knighty and Youngy stand opposite each other, Darcy is
the ref.*

46

Off we go then, lads. We'll have three one-minute
rounds.

*The two approach each other, Knighty throws a careless
punch, Youngy easily avoids and follows through with an
uppercut that sends Knighty to the floor.*

                    KNIGHTY
You cheeky fuckin' knob.

*Knighty yanks off his gloves and runs at Youngy, kicking him
and throwing his arms out wildly. The camera hand-held and
frantic, follows Darcy as he jumps in the ring, grabs Knighty
and throws him to the floor. He then pushes him out of the
ring. He climbs through the ropes, grabs Knighty and manhandles him out of the building.*

                    DARCY
                 (*as he goes*)
Right, next pair start. Tim, you ref, any more of that sort
of crap in the ring and I'll personally ensure that you
walk with a limp from this day on.

36 INT. BOXING CLUB – DAY

*The scene moves to outside the building. Darcy has Knighty
pinned against the wall.*

                    DARCY
Well?

                    KNIGHTY
Well what?

Knighty is furious and close to tears.

                    DARCY
Did you hear a word of what I said before you started
then?

47

Fuck off!

Did ya, did ya, a?

He is shaking Knighty.

Did ya hear one single word?

Knighty lets out a furious scream and knees Darcy in the bollocks. Darcy reaches into his pants and pulls out a cricket box.

I'm wearing one of these, you dirty little scumbag.

Darcy steps back, takes off his shirt and puts up his fists.

Right, you think you're a big man, you talk like one, don't you! So put your hands up and let's sort this out once and for all. Queensbury's out of the window now, come on. Come on, I'll wipe you all over this path. I mean it!

Knighty is silenced and very scared.

If you're gonna come here then I want respect. There's no room for that sort of crap you showed then, d'ya understand?

Knighty nods.

Good lad, now go back inside and no kicking and I tell you, if you do any more of that, I'll break your arm.

Darcy has calmed down.

You'd be doing me a favour, me old man would stop trying to make me get a job.

Knighty walks back inside. Fagash is walking back.

Alright, Wesley, no offence, mate.

FAGASH
None taken, Darcy. It was shit weed anyway.

37 INT. BOXING CLUB – DAY

The scene cuts to back in the ring. Daz and Benny are fighting. Daz is pissed off by Benny's skill; he is made to look rubbish. The beginnings of a fight erupt. Benny knocks out Daz's gumshield. The Lads are all cheering. Revenge is being taken for the hot sausage in the eye. Daz looks to Knighty for help. None is given. Benny is easily beating him. The bell rings.

Darcy is sitting on a work bench writing in his diary; around him we see the Lads sparring or watching. Fagash is standing in the doorway smoking a spliff.

38 EXT. BOXING CLUB – DAY

The scene changes to Darcy locking the door to the hall, as he walks away a group of kids run past him, they are dressed in soldier outfits. One of them is heard to comment on Darcy along the lines of: 'There's that weird bloke.' We fade to black.

39 EXT. TRAIN STATION SHELTER – DAY

Darcy is painting the shelter. We see him cleaning for a short while. Into the scene enters Ronnie and his son Tonka. Tonka is a chubby lad.

RONNIE
Alright there, Darcy. Don't stop, san, bought me boy darn to meet ya. Tonka, this is Darcy.

TONKA
(*dull-voiced*)

I know.

DARCY

Hello there. Tonka your real name?

TONKA

No.

RONNIE

It's 'is nickname 'cause 'e's fat, int that right, Tonks?

TONKA

Yer.

RONNIE

Look, Darcy, I'll be straight wiv ya, boy. You know his mum left us, right? Well I went further into the business, working crazy hours, you know, as a way of escaping. Tonka on the other hand started eating, all the fucking time, you know, it was a fucking cry for help. I weren't there, was I? And now I'm seeing this new bird, right? I know that I can put it all right again. But Tonka won't let her in. He still loves his old mum. And she's really trying. When I heard about this club, I just fought, if you could train him and get him to lose a bit of weight, his confidence will come back. Me and his new mum can come to all the matches and we can start to put our life into some kind of order. What do you say? Can he come?

DARCY

Well, I suppose it won't do no harm.

RONNIE

Ya see, ma boy, I put sam of me extra cash inta this fing Darcy's doin' for you lot, so, in my heart, I know that he'll look arfter ya. No what am sayin', boy?

TONKA

Yer.

RONNIE

Right, you stay here and help out Mr Darcy with his paintin'. Get those lessons started early, boy.

TONKA

OK.

Ronnie leaves.

DARCY

May as well pass me that tub of paint then, Tonka.

TONKA

Ma real name's Karl.

Tonka drops a tin of paint over himself as he is passing it to Darcy.

40 INT. POOL HALL – DAY

The scene is set in a twenty-four-hour pool hall. We can see all of the Lads playing pool around one table. They are playing doubles for money. Gadget and Knighty are losing to Fagash and Meggy. Daz is sitting watching because his Giro still hasn't arrived.

The pool hall is smoky; a few people are playing on other tables. The first thing we see is Meggy doing a trick shot.

FAGASH

May as well pot the black straight off shag.

KNIGHTY

No way, it's not over until the fat lady sings.

DAZ
(*holding arms out to represent a fat belly, singing like a tenor*)
I'm a fat lump of lard, hear my juice tune as you loose.

More laughter.

KNIGHTY

Someone hit him. Get Benny to 'it 'im.

Everyone laughs except Daz. Knighty turns his attention to two Lads on the table next to theirs.

Lads, do us a favour and hit that bloke there for us.

STUDENT 1

Sorry?

KNIGHTY

It's alright.

Knighty takes a shot. He misses.

FAGASH

Left it lovely for me there, Knighty.

He takes a shot and pots the ball.

KNIGHTY
(*knowing he's lost, he turns his attention to the two Lads on the other table*)
So where you two from?

STUDENT 1

Conway, in Wales.

KNIGHTY

Sheep-shagger, ah?

STUDENT 1

No, we only moved there a couple of years ago.

KNIGHTY

So you're not from there, then?

STUDENT 1

Yer, but not originally.

KNIGHTY

Don't get cocky, mate.

STUDENT 1

I'm not.

KNIGHTY

Think you're a big man, ah? A bet you're a friggin'
student?

STUDENT 1

Yer, we are.

KNIGHTY

What you learnin'?

STUDENT 1

Am doin' creative arts.

KNIGHTY

That's basket-weavin', innit? So what's your boyfriend,
doin'?

STUDENT 1

He's not my boyfriend.

KNIGHTY

Arr, had a row, have we?

DAZ

You've got about eight games' worth of twenty pences
on there. Want to play doubles?

STUDENT 2

I've got to get an essay in soon.

KNIGHTY

Ooo, he speaks, I thought you were dumb or something.

DAZ

I heard them say you were a wanker a minute ago.

                    STUDENT I
No we didn't.

                    DAZ
You calling me a liar?

                    STUDENT I
No.

                    DAZ
So you did call my mate a wanker?

                    STUDENT I
No, look we didn't say anything.

                    KNIGHTY
Only pissing around, lads. Look we'll play you then, ah?
Quid a corner?

                    STUDENT I
                    (*resigned*)
Alright then.

                    KNIGHTY
Right, lads, this is my mate Sue and his girlfriend Sarah.

They all laugh, the Students look nervous.

*We see Daz put the cash into the table. A musical sequence
begins – 'Till the Groove' by Gavin Clarke. We see a series of
shots from a number of games. Images of the Lads laughing,
the two Students looking scared, Daz threatening, shots being
taken, breaks, the Students with a tray of drinks passing them
around the Lads, crashing fags, et cetera.*

*As the scene continues we notice that the other Lads leave.
Daz, Knighty and the Students continue playing.*

41 EXT. POOL HALL – DAY

*The scene cuts to the entrance of the pool hall. All four walk
out. By the doorway are two mountain bikes.*

DAZ

So which one is yours then, Sue?

STUDENT 2

That one.

DAZ

Yer, that'll do. Nice one, lads.

KNIGHTY

Cheers for the games then, girls. Might see you next
week.

*Knighty gets onto the back of the mountain bike and they
ride away. Student 2 is seen to push Student 1. The scene fades
out.*

42 INT. JO'S SHOP – DAY

*Darcy has to hide his disappointment at various stages. He
does this by asking offbeat questions. This is the first time we
see a lack of confidence in Darcy.*

DARCY

Hello there, Jo, I just popped in for the corner cushions.

JO
(*smiling*)

I'm getting there . . . How's the club doing?

DARCY

Great, come down tomorrow and I'll give you a guided
tour.

JO

I've got to help my mum find some curtains tomorrow.

DARCY
(*covering over a small amount of disappointment
with this gem*)

Which room's she getting the curtains for?

JO

They're not actually for my mum, they're for me nan's
new bungalow.

DARCY
(*pause, awkward*)
Oh right, she's in that new block, isn't she?

JO
(*laughing*)
Yeah. She's after all the men.

DARCY
What is it then, like a complex?

JO
Yeah. We call it Club 80.

DARCY
That sounds great. I'll be there myself in the not to
distant future. This boxing has already taken the final
strands of youth from my cranium.

*She laughs. Darcy waits for her to dispel what he has just said
with a compliment . . .She doesn't. Long pause. Jo laughs.*

*Darcy looks around the shop briefly and chooses a huge box of
chocolates from the display.*

Well, I'll take that and go about my business.

*Darcy smiles and tries to join in on her laugh, but there is a
look of hurt and confusion on his face. He pays for the
chocolates with a twenty-pound note and as he walks past the
camera he closes his eyes, shakes his head and looks silently
pissed off.*

43 INT. BOXING CLUB – DAY

*The Lads are all sitting in the doorway of the club, all of them
smoking fags. The camera will highlight the amount of*

smoking that is going on. Through the door we can see Darcy is brushing the ring – the camera tracks in on Darcy, he is seen to sing into the brush and dance.

Darcy sings . . .

DARCY

Come on, let's get back to work.

The Lads throw their fag-ends down and walk back in.

I've got us another medicine ball by the way.

KNIGHTY

What we gonna use Tonka for now?

TONKA

Why's everyone keep pickin' on me?

DARCY

'Cause you let them.

We cut to a bit later on in the session. Darcy is standing over Tonka with a medicine ball. He drops it.

TONKA

Arrrhh . . . Ya hit me in me appendix.

The Lads are laughing.

Get lost!

Tonka stands up, swinging around violently.

Come on, yer bastards.

DARCY

Tonka, calm, lad. It's meant to hurt ya, it makes the fat stronger. Ya can't go like that in the ring. Someone hits you in ya fat gut you'll no breathe again till next week.

He playfully squeezes at Tonka's chubby belly. The Lads join in, some squeezing his arse, others rubbing his head.

57

Knighty and Daz are seen standing on the street outside the gym. It is after the training session. They are waiting for a taxi to go to get hash from Fagash.

The taxi pulls up. Knighty gets in the front, Daz in the back.

45 INT. TAXI – DAY

The scene cuts to inside the car. The driver is about forty-five, Irish and slightly drunk.

> KNIGHTY
>
> Saint Thomas Court please, mate.

> TAXI DRIVER
>
> Right, Lads. Sorry I'm a bit late, like. I left the pub without me keys, and we all know that you can't drink and drive without keys.

There is a look of general fear on the Lads' faces. There is a long pause, until Daz pipes up with a weather comment to calm the atmosphere.

> DAZ
>
> It's gone cold of late, hasn't it?

> TAXI DRIVER
>
> Sorry, that's me, that is. I've just wound my window down.

Knighty laughs.

> DAZ
>
> No. I meant . . .

He laughs as well.

The taxi pulls away then slams to a halt after about half a minute. The Driver turns up the radio – the lottery announcer is reading out the numbers. The Driver reaches over Knighty's

legs to the glove compartment. He opens it and takes out a lottery ticket.

TAXI DRIVER
What were those last three numbers?

KNIGHTY
Don't know, mate. Why, have you won?

TAXI DRIVER
Don't know yet.

DAZ
I heard twenty-four, thirty-eight and twelve.

TAXI DRIVER
Yer, you see I've got them . . .

RADIO
And here they are again in numerical order . . .

KNIGHTY
Can we have a free ride if you win?

TAXI DRIVER
Shhh . . .

RADIO
Number one, number eight, number twelve, number twenty-four, number twenty-five, number thirty-six.

TAXI DRIVER
Fuckin' hell, I've got five.

RADIO
And the bonus ball is thirty-eight.

TAXI DRIVER
Yes, yes. Jeysus yes . . .

The Driver bashes his car horn, he hugs Knighty, turns round and celebrates in Daz's face. He's jumping round in his seat unable to control his excitement.

Shit shit shit shits shit . . .

KNIGHTY
I can't believe this. You sure, mate . . .?

TAXI DRIVER
Yer, look.

He shows Knighty the numbers, making sure not to let go of the ticket.

KNIGHTY
He fuckin' has as well, Daz.

DAZ
So can we have a free ride then, mate?

TAXI DRIVER
You can have her full stop, Lads.

He opens the door and gets out, then leans back in.

I can't believe this, the wife'll have a fuckin' heart attack. Am away to the pub.

He skips and jumps out of sight; the Lads sit in silence for a minute.

46 EXT. POLICE STATION – DAY

Darcy is seen to exit with Daz and Knighty, who have been locked away for the night after being stopped driving the cab. They exit and walk up the street.

DARCY
I gave them a list of your names and asked them to call me if any of you were down here.

KNIGHTY
That's like one of those scary futuristic movies.

DAZ

He'll be having us tagged next.

KNIGHTY

I don't know, you try and go straight and some bloke just gives you a car. I can't believe it. What a mare.

DARCY

Yer, what a mare, I was supposed to be helping a friend today. How do you fancy earning a football, lads?

DAZ

You must be joking, I havn'e slept all night.

KNIGHTY

The last time anyone got offered footballs they had to paint the station shelter for the day

DARCY

It's probably too late now anyway.

KNIGHTY

Good.

47 INT. BOXING CLUB – DAY

Darcy and all the Lads are sitting in a group. They have just come to the end of a session and all are looking worn out and sweaty.

DARCY

Right, a couple of things, lads. First of all, the next person I pick up from the police is out, OK? Two months and that's the first brush with the law we've seen.

KNIGHTY

That's not bad, is it?

DARCY

No, not bad at all. It means that we can push on with plans.

KNIGHTY

What plans?

DARCY

I think we should have a match against another club.

GADGET

When . . . ?

DARCY

A month or so. I've been to the papers and they're going to publish an article about us. There's a bloke coming in a bit to take our picture.

The Lads are quiet.

So start combing your hair.

BENNY

Got your comb, Tonka?

He rubs Tonka's skinhead.

TONKA

Funny.

DARCY

Also, Tonka's dad has put some money into the club to get us off the ground, which is good, don't you think?

The Lads clap and whistle with minimal enthusiasm.

Best of all though, we've got enough kitty money to go away for a few days.

Darcy is getting enthusiastic; the Lads are quiet.

DARCY

Lads, we're going to Wales.

The Lads are silent.

Well, don't get too excited.

KNIGHTY
(*an aside to Daz*)
We'll probably meet up with those fuckin' students.

Daz laughs.

DARCY
Come on, Lads, it'll be great, a chance to fully concentrate your minds and have a break as well. Get it together for the match.

STUART
(*disapprovingly*)
For how long?

DARCY
A couple of days

GADGET
Is it free?

DARCY
Yes.

Gadget smiles.

Right, so that's that. 10 a.m., Saturday, meet here. By the way, two rules. No pot, no lady friends and no drink after midnight.

The Lads begin to moan we hear things like 'That was three things' and 'No way'.

A Photographer walks in. He has hair hanging over his eyes and trips over a barbell, then stumbles before slipping on water by the side of the ring. He bangs into the ring as he falls, this knocks over a bucket of water which was balanced on the edge of the ring. The Lads and Darcy are laughing.

PHOTOGRAPHER
(*looking at his wet camera*)
Oh fuck, I was going to say let's do it outside before it
rains, but it doesn't matter now.

Fits of laughing as we fade to black.

48 EXT. BOXING CLUB – DAY

*Darcy and all the Lads except Tonka and Gadget have
arrived. It is the Saturday morning. We see bags lying in a
pile on the floor and the Lads standing around smoking fags.
Darcy looks tired and pissed off. He's looking at his watch
and then down the road.*

DARCY
Transport is arriving, Lads.

*The Lads gather in anticipation of a bus. An old rusty-looking
Transit van pulls up in front of them.*

Don't worry, Lads, there's a few cushions in the back.

KNIGHTY
We're going all the way to Wales in the back of that?

DARCY
Don't be such a wet bum.

*Ronnie's car pulls up behind the van. We see Tonka get out
and open the boot of the car, he takes out three big bags.
Ronnie gets out. He goes to the boot, and gives Tonka a slap
across the head. Ronnie then puts two of the bags back into
the car and gives Tonka the third. Then Ronnie's new
'missus' (Sharon) gets out dressed in mini skirt, heels, etc. She
begins an argument about how many bags Tonka needs.
Everyone stands around baffled as this takes place.*

SHARON
He can't go with one bag. I've packed five. And there's

essential things spread out amongst them.

                    RONNIE
Leave it out, you ain't supposed to rebuild your
bedroom when you get there are you, Tonka?

Tonka shrugs.

See. It ain't about comforts and stuff, it's about bonding
and living in a different environment and all that.

                    SHARON
It's not that easy now though, is it?

                    RONNIE
Why?

                    SHARON
Morning, night. There isn't one bag with an even
mixture of things in it. The bag you're giving him has
only got pyjamas in it.

                    RONNIE
Facking 'ell. Well, how many do you want to take, son?

                    TONKA
Three.

                    SHARON
He'll need at least three.

                    RONNIE
Three it is then.

*Tonka, the lad who started out with three bags, sighs a very
heavy sigh. Then he and Ronnie walk over to the group.*

Al'rite there, boys, lookin' in good nick there, doin'
alright are we then, ah?

A few of the Lads mumble, fine, etc.

Alan, quick word in your ear-like thing.

The two men convene away from the Lads. Ronnie gives Darcy an envelope.

Seventy nicka there, Alan. Now you give these boys a good workin' for me, ah, Alan? Av written me mobile on there, look, ya? Just in case, alright?

DARCY

Alright, Ronnie, cheers a lot, mate.

We hear the Lads cheering. Ronnie and Darcy turn to see that Gadget is bobbling along with a big bin liner over his shoulder. He reaches the group.

GADGET

Sorry am late, I couldn't find a proper bag for me stuff.

Everyone laughs. The scene moves forward a bit. We see everyone standing around the back of the van. Darcy opens up the blind-style door.

DARCY

In we get, Lads. By the way, am gonna do a bag check when we get there to see if you've all complied with the rules.

Darcy walks round to the front of the van. As he does this we see the Lads taking the booze out of their bags and stuffing it up their jackets. They get into the van and begin arguing about who is sitting where. We, the camera, stay in wide shot outside the van as this argument takes place for a short while. We then hear Darcy scream, 'Sit down,' and the van finally pulls away. We fade to black and the music begins. The pace in the following sequences covering their stay in Wales aims to elucidate the calming effect and the bonding process that takes place between Darcy and the Lads during this stay in Wales through a series of beautifully composed wide shots.

49 EXT. SHOPS — DAY

Shopping . . .

50 EXT. FIELDS — DAY

Running up hills . . .

51 INT. HUT — NIGHT

Asleep in their bunks while Darcy writes in his diary. Darcy and the Lads are like a swan and her cygnets swimming closely behind in every scene. As the music fades we cut to the riverbank scene.

52 EXT. STREAM — WALES — DAY

We see the Lads spread along the bank of the stream, fishing with their home-made rods; we see lots of laughing and smiling.

Darcy is sat with Tim, surrounded by tackle. Darcy is sitting on a fold-out chair; Tim is sitting on a tackle box. Darcy pours them both a cup of coffee from his flask.

>   TIM
> This is good, Darcy. It's nice to get away.

>   DARCY
> That's the old sayin' about changes a suppose.

>   TIM
> You feel sorry for me, don't you?

>   DARCY
> I feel sorry for the blindness you have to your situation.

There is silence while the two cast their rods into the water.

>   TIM
> It's not a blindness, Darcy.

DARCY

I know that, Tim. You're not the only one going through a bad time.

TIM

Whatever.

Darcy takes out a flask.

DARCY

Here ya go, mate. Nice cup of Fireside blend.

TIM

That's the shit that Fagash buys.

DARCY

Don't knock Kwik Save, my friend.

Tim casts his line; he overestimates and it lands on the other side of the bank.

TIM

Ooh, shit . . .

DARCY

Bit of an overcast.

TIM

A bit of one, that maggot's goin' straight to casualty, mate. It'll have a sling and be on crutches for the next few months.

Both laugh again.

Tim goes over the bridge to untangle his line.

Back in a minute.

After sitting alone for a while Darcy begins to sing.

DARCY

The closer I get, the further I fall. I'm counting on you not to make me fall, I need your love like I need a bite.

So come on baby throw me a line. Tra la la-la-la, tra la la-la-la. Tra la la-la-la, I want to have the fishin' crown.

As the ditty ends, we see a close-up of the float splashing into the water. Back into shot of Darcy as Tim arrives back.

DARCY

Here we go, here we go . . . Look there she goes . . .

Tim grabs the net and moves into position beside Darcy.

TIM

It's a big 'un, it's putting' up a right fight. Come on, baby. Slowly does it . . . In she comes. Look, look. Did ya see that, did ya see it?

The men are acting like kids at Christmas.

DARCY

I did, I did, right, drop the net down now. Come on, my lovely.

The fish gets away.

Oh balls . . . That was a bloody monster, did ya see it?

TIM

It wasn't his time.

We see a shot of the whole group from the other side of the river. They are seen to do a Mexican wave and chant 'Come on you fish'. As the camera observes this, Darcy begins a short voice-over.

DARCY
(*voice-over*)

We sit and watch our floats. In calm water it is still and tranquil; in rough water it shifts around, ducking and weaving. It's the sport of kings and labourers. There's no class, except the quality of your maggot.

The sun is setting, we see that Darcy is asleep.

TIM

Darcy . . .

DARCY
(*waking from a dream*)
Don't trust the pigs to rule you. Shoot the bloody pig
first.

TIM
(*laughing*)
I think the Lads are getting bored. We should pack up
and go home.

We see shots of the Lads sword-fighting with the rods.

DARCY
(*still half asleep*)
Mmm . . . yep.

We see the Lads packing up their rods.

(*voice-over*)
As a child my dad would tell me a story before bed. He'd
say that if the earth was a big floating ball, ten foot by ten
foot, which was surrounded by gas that held the water in
place, then people would come from everywhere to see
this amazing sight. They would stare in awe at the
beauty. And when they looked at it with a magnifying
glass, they would see people moving around, they would
be overcome with wonderment at these tiny creatures.

53 INT. VAN – DAY

*We cut to a shot inside the van of Darcy driving with the
Lads asleep in the background.*

DARCY
(*voice-over*)
And then he'd say that I was one of these tiny creatures; I
was special and wonderful, everything I did was a miracle.

71

When I remember this I feel on top of the world. On our way home from Wales we were a boxing club on the verge of our first clash – that made me feel the same way.

Fade to black.

54 EXT. JO'S SHOP – DAY

Darcy pulls up in his Reliant Robin.

55 INT. JO'S SHOP – DAY

In this scene we get the feeling that Darcy kind of likes Jo. Through his fumbled speech he asks her out. She does not really realise that he is aiming at a date.

DARCY

Hello there, Jo.

JO

Hiya. How was Wales?

DARCY

Magic. It's made a big impact on the Lads.

Darcy looks at the magazine stand.

JO

A lot of people have seen the article. Everyone is talking about it.

Pause.

DARCY

Oh magic . . . You haven't forgotten to save me some for the Lads, have you?

JO

I saved you one. The Lads were all outside me shop this morning at five-thirty. Gadget was in his pyjamas, dressing-gown and a pair of fishing wellies.

Jo hands Darcy the paper. He reads quickly over the article.
Jo proceeds to put some fags on the display behind her.

> DARCY
>
> It's nice. It's a shame they didn't mention Ronnie. I told
> 'em he was sponsoring it. Nice though, int it?

> JO
>
> It's great.

> DARCY
>
> How was your mother?

> JO
>
> Claustrophobic.

She laughs.

> DARCY
>
> I don't want to be impertinent, like, but would you
> fancy a drink maybe to make up for it?
>   (*pause*)
> Friday night?
>   (*uncomfortable pause*)
> After the training?

Jo is slightly taken aback. She just looks at him.

> JO
>
> Erm . . .

> DARCY
>   (*back to the drawing-board*)
> Just to talk about the ring cushions and all that.

Darcy is bright red. Jo is bright red.

> JO
>
> Alright.

Darcy clicks his heels and leaves. As he walks past the camera
we see him close his eyes and mouth the words shit, shit.

Meggy is sitting having tea with his girlfriend, Lesley. They are eating fish fingers and chips. Meggy's girlfriend never goes out with him when he's with the Lads; she knows that they're a bad influence. People are of the general opinion that she is far too good for him; Meggy doesn't give a shit.

MEGGY

What's the problem?

LESLEY

The problem is that everybody in the town is laughing at you. It's only you and your stupid mates who's taking it seriously.

MEGGY

Well thanks a lot, Lesley!

He stands up and walks away. As he goes he shouts.

I really appreciate your support.

He thinks of something that will make her feel guilty and turns back.

I've got a match coming up soon, I'm probably gonna get my teeth knocked out and I get all this grief come home.

LESLEY

What about your fish fingers?

He stops at the door and turns to her.

MEGGY

What about 'em? They're shit. If I eat another fish finger I'll turn into Captain Bird's-Eye.

He slams the door and leaves.

57 INT. KNIGHTY'S HOUSE – KITCHEN – DAY

Knighty and his Mum and Dad are sitting in their kitchen. They too are eating fish fingers and chips. Knighty's Dad, Adrian, is reading the article. Knighty and his Mum are looking anxious as they wait for his verdict.

> KNIGHTY
>
> What d'ya think then, Dad?

> ADRIAN
>
> It seems like quite a good article, son. Looks like you're all enjoying it as well.

> JANET
> (*looks to her son*)
>
> I just think it's nice to have you in there for something good, duck. I'll go and get a copy of the photo tomorrow and stick it in the scrap book.

> ADRIAN
> (*puts the paper down*)
>
> It's a shame they didn't write about any of our club's fights. There would be no comparison. Only joking, son. I'm really proud of ya.

He pats Knighty on the back and then they all begin to eat their tea.

58 INT. TIM'S HOUSE – KITCHEN – DAY

Tim and his parents are sitting at the table in their kitchen symbolically eating fish fingers and chips. Woody the dog is eating food out of a bowl, next to Tim. Hand-held camera.

> GEOFF
>
> Ideas above your station. You've always been the same. I suppose being in the papers with a group of monkeys makes you feel great, don't it?

TIM

Leave us alone, Dad.

His Dad slams his hand down on the table.

GEOFF

Watch your trap! Boy!

He goes to slap Tim. Tim grabs his arm.

TIM

Get your hands off me!

Tim stands up.

Why can't you just be happy for me? You have to ruin everything.

Geoff very calmly takes a cigarette from his packet, lights it, and puts it in the ashtray.

GEOFF

You ever raise your hand to me again, son, and you'll never walk through that front door again. Just think about your mother and what all this is doing to her.

Pat is crying. Tim is standing with his fists clenched. Geoff stands up, looks at Tim and leaves the room. Although he seems cool and calm he has backed down for the first time.

I'm going to the pub.

59 INT. BENNY'S HOUSE – LIVING ROOM – DAY

Benny is sitting in his living room with Youngy and Stuart. Benny is making fish finger sandwiches. These are no ordinary fish fingers though. These are Bird's-Eye Prime Cod Steak in Batter Gold.

YOUNGY

They're alright the Lads, really.

BENNY

Me mum's not too keen on me hanging around with
them.

STUART

Darcy reckons he can straighten them out.

YOUNGY

Darcy's an idiot.

BENNY

He's not.

YOUNGY

'Cause he is, he's pushing things too quickly. I mean, the
article makes us out to be future champs. He's pushing
things too quickly.

BENNY

You just don't get it do you, Youngy?

YOUNGY

What?

Benny and Stuart ignore him.

What did I say?

60 INT. FAGASH'S FLAT – FRONT ROOM – DAY

*Daz and Gadget are sitting in Fagash's front room. They
have about twenty copies of the paper lying about. Guess
what? They are eating fish fingers and chips. Gadget is still
wearing his pyjamas and wellies.*

DAZ

Have you got any stamps, Fagash?

FAGASH

No . . . What d'ya want stamps for?

78

DAZ

I wanna send that girl in Doncaster a copy of the article. You know, the one I met at Alton Towers.

GADGET

That's the one that finished with ya, int it?

DAZ

Yer, this'll show er. She said I'd never go anywhere.

He admires the article.

GADGET

It's not exactly mass press, is it?

DAZ

I've only ever been in the paper after I've been in court before.

GADGET
(*spitting out some fish finger*)
Fagash, are these value fingers?

FAGASH

Nah man, they're economy ones.

GADGET

I told ya to get decent ones. They only have about a three per cent fish in these things.

FAGASH

If ya don't like 'em, get out me house.

GADGET

I gave ya the two quid for 'em, you've only paid about fifty pence for these.

DAZ

Oh yes, sorry.

Daz bursts out laughing.

We fade up from black and see Darcy pulling weeds up from the sides of the alley. He is wearing khaki-coloured shorts, a vest and a big floppy white hat. He sticks the weeds in a bin bag and walks to the end of the alley to put them in a bin. We hear a car driving up; it stops next to Darcy and beeps its horn, which makes him jump a mile and drop the weeds all over the floor. The back door to the car opens and we hear a voice from inside. Ronnie's name has not appeared in the article and he is upset.

RONNIE

Cam 'ere, Darcy!

DARCY

Alright, Ronnie. Is it about the paper? I did tell them to mention you.

A hand reaches out, grabs Darcy's arm and pulls him into the car. As he is pulled in he bangs his head very firmly on the top of the car. He immediately drops to the floor unconscious – half in the car, half out. Ronnie leans forward. He tries to pull Darcy's large unconscious body inside.

RONNIE
(heaving)

Fack me . . . Hrummm. He weighs a ton. Oh god, I didn't want to hurt him.

Talking to his 'missus', Sharon.

Get out and help me get him in. His facking head's bleedin'. We'd better get him to the hospital.

They both heave and try to load him in.

His bones must be made out of friggin' lead.

SHARON

What did you do that for, you bloody bully?

RONNIE

I didn't do it on purpose, did I?

Sharon just glares at him. Ronnie cowers.

62 INT. HOSPITAL – CASUALTY WAITING AREA – DAY

Darcy is sitting next to Ronnie. Darcy has a lot of blood around his face. He is holding a large surgical sponge to his forehead: Ronnie is reading Marie Claire. *Darcy looks really confused and quite lost, he is sipping coffee but it is missing his mouth and dribbling down onto his bloody shirt. Sharon takes the coffee from Darcy and places it on the floor.*

RONNIE

You alright there, Darcy? You look a bit of a knock there, son.

He points to the fruit bowl on the chair next to Darcy.

I got you some satsumas . . .

Darcy just looks at him.

I'm sorry about your 'ead. It was an accident.

Darcy turns to look at Ronnie.

Oh no, look at yar. It won't mess fings up, will it, Darce? I was really upset about the article. I thought we were partners.

DARCY

I told her to mention you, though.

RONNIE

Cam on, don't be a mardy bum.

DARCY

You nearly cracked my skull open. I did tell her to mention your name, Ronnie. You know what they're

81

like. I'd have thought you would have been happy that we got any kind of good review.

> RONNIE
> What do ya want me to say? I'm sorry . . . it was an accident I only wanted to talk to ya, honest. I overreacted. Don't let's stop being mates. Cam on, put it there, partner.

Ronnie puts out his hand.

> DARCY
> I can't put it there, 'cause it's holding me bandage on.

> RONNIE
> Well shake wiv the other hand then.

> DARCY
> It doesn't count if it's left-handed.

> RONNIE
> Well, let me hold the bandage wiv me left and then you can shake.

> DARCY
> Just forget the handshake, Ronnie. I'll do it later.

Ronnie looks upset. A Nurse approaches and takes Darcy off to get his wound dressed. Ronnie turns to the old guy on his left.

> RONNIE
> Excuse me, do you know if a handshake with your left hand counts?

Sharon shakes her head in disbelief.

63 INT. IRIS'S HOUSE – FRONT ROOM – DAY

Darcy calls on Iris, his aunty, after training. She has a very simple, clean house, with scattered photos on the walls of

Darcy and other family members seen in the title sequence. There is a range of ticking clocks and an upright piano in the corner. Darcy and Iris sit down with a cup of tea. Iris is slightly hard of hearing.

> DARCY
>
> How's your knee?

> IRIS
> *(having a sip of tea)*
> Lovely thanks. It'll be better for a bit of dancing on Wednesday. How did you get on in Wales?

> DARCY
>
> Fine.

> IRIS
>
> You seem a bit down.

> DARCY
>
> I'm fine, Iris, really. I've just got to meet with the Mayor tomorrow and the match is coming up next week.

> IRIS
>
> Well don't overdo it, Alan, or you'll be gone quicker than your uncle George.

Darcy removes his coat and goes into the hall to hang it up.

The scene moves forward. Iris is sitting at the piano. Darcy is leaning on it smoking a Cuban cigar. They have had a couple of sherries apiece. They are singing quite liberally. Thirty seconds later we hear a megamix of songs we think we've heard but can't quite make out. Although slightly comical, it is quite beautiful in its innocence and conviction. Fade to black.

64 INT. MAYOR'S OFFICE – DAY

We fade up to see Darcy sitting opposite the Mayor at his desk. They are in the middle of an argument. Quite heated.

MAYOR

What are you tryin' to do here? Don't you see the
leftovers from your day cluttered around our pubs. I
want direction in this town, that's why we back the race
course and the industrial estates and the housing
developments.

*Darcy is controlling his anger, trying to remain calm, as he
knows rage will have him thrown out.*

DARCY

You can't build a super-structure if your infrastructure is
falling to bits. It'll just slowly destroy everything, like
bad damping. Each of us has leisure time. Some too
much, that's the cause of this violent society. All I'm
asking is for you to show up, man. Give them a chance.
What is your problem?

MAYOR
(shouting back)
It's illegal. It isn't 1972, Alan. You have no certification.
You have no recognised training. You really think that a
group of robbers are going to get support from me? I'll
have to get police protection for anyone who goes to the
stupid gimmick.

DARCY

You're talking out of your arse, but that's fine, you're
just small-scale, so it should be expected, I suppose.
You're not going to stop this match though, as long as
you know that.

MAYOR

Just get out.

Darcy leaves.

We see the Lads training. After a short period Darcy blows a
whistle and calls the Lads together. Darcy is wearing a few
bandages from his earlier escapade.

DARCY

We're nearly there now, Lads. That article was a stepping
stone into the public's arms, and we crossed it well. You
all realise that a front-page headline means we'll
probably get a really good crowd for this first match.
Tonka's dad has put up the money for the match. We'll
show the Mayor who needs crutches.

KNIGHTY

What's with the stupid Scooby Doo riddles, Darcy?
Why wasn't we quoted or anything?

DARCY

It was about publicity and individually you lot don't
make good publicity . . . Areas of interest, that's what
they're looking for. Everyone in town is talking about
us.

DAZ

Am no bein' no prawn for anyone.

BENNY

Prawn?

A few Lads laugh.

DAZ

Pawn, a mean. Same shit anyway, innit Lads?

GADGET

I still don't think I'm ready for all this. I'm still coughing
up car engines.

DARCY

Don't talk soft. Don't pull out on me now. This is

exactly why the authorities won't help us. I know you're capable of being something. Just enjoy this time. I'll give you all a chance to leave now if you want.

Everyone stops.

Right, one thing before we start. Where's the first aid kit?

Everyone looks around the room.

And has anyone seen Fagash in the last few days?

KNIGHTY
You should have spent more time on the basics at school, Darcy.

Laughter.

66 INT. POOL HALL – DAY

Both groups of Lads are sat around a couple of benches pulled together (Benny, Knighty, Daz, Gadget, Meggy, Tim, Youngy, and Stuart). There are a number of conversations happening. Everyone is drinking lots of beer. They have just finished training with Darcy. They seem a lot more like a club since the trip to Wales.

KNIGHTY
Not this particular mayor, he got sacked for smackin' this kid at my dad's school in the sixties.

YOUNGY
The kid was probably out of order.

KNIGHTY
Probably wouldn't wear the leather pants.

DAZ
Wales was cool, man. I'm gonna write to the chick in the pie shop.

86

STUART

What about your girlfriend?

DAZ

Yeah but that's this port.

He laughs alone.

KNIGHTY

He won't help Darcy out 'cause of us lot.

DAZ

The Mayor don't do shit, man.

KNIGHTY

We should try and shaft the Mayor, Lads. Why don't we photograph him in bed in his wildlife snake pants? And then we can bribe him, a touch.

DAZ

I'm up for that.

BENNY

What, you gonna do sneak to his house, climb the wall and take pictures?

KNIGHTY

We're all doin' it.
                    (*to everyone*)
Right Lads, mission on.

67 EXT. FAGASH'S HOUSE – DAY

Darcy bangs on the door of Fagash's house.

68 EXT. FAGASH'S HOUSE – HALL – DAY

We cut to the inside view of the front door as Darcy continues to bang the letter box and shout; the camera pulls away into the lounge. We see Darcy force open the door and walk towards camera.

69 INT. FAGASH'S HOUSE – LIVING ROOM – DAY

Once in the lounge he stops and stares, out of view. We cut to a shot of Fagash. He is slumped back in his armchair, semi-conscious. Vomit is dribbling from his mouth, on his lap is some silver foil and in his hand is a fag-shaped rolled-up piece of foil.

Darcy crouches beside him, holding his head by the chin and shaking him softly. He is talking in a quiet relaxed manner.

> DARCY
> What are you doing, ah? What are you, Wesley? What are you doing?

Fagash's eyes are beyond his control. He coughs.

> Look at ya, Wesley. I don't tell you, do I?

70 INT. FAGASH'S HOUSE – BATHROOM – DAY

The scene moves forward as we see Darcy putting Fagash in the shower, helping him to clean himself up.

71 INT. FAGASH'S HOUSE – BEDROOM – DAY

Darcy puts Fagash to bed.

72 INT. FAGASH'S HOUSE – BEDROOM – DAY

We see Darcy cleaning up the house and preparing some soup.

73 EXT. SUBURBAN HOUSING ESTATE – NIGHT

We see the whole group of Lads walking up the street, led by Knighty. The rest of the Lads have fallen into place behind him. Gadget and Meggy are carrying a ladder. They stop outside a house and all duck behind a row of ferns that shades the house. They all shush each other.

KNIGHTY

Right, someone holds the ladder, someone takes the
picture and someone bangs on his door to wake him up
so we can get a shot of his tackle.

MEGGY

I'm not doin' anythin' else, I ripped my shirt gettin' the
ladder.

GADGET

Me neither, I carried it.

*The Lads mumble about who's going to do what, then begin
the mission. Daz and Benny carry the ladder to the house and
carefully prop it against the wall. Knighty slowly climbs the
ladder. He gives the thumbs up to Daz, who waves his arms
at the group assembled in the driveway. Tim is pushed
forward. He goes to the door. He bangs the letter box.*

TIM

It's an emergency, we need the Mayor. We need the
Mayor.

*All the Lads duck back behind the ferns; Tim runs to join
them.*

KNIGHTY
(*whispering*)

He didn't hear you, try again.

TIM

Fuckin' hell.

*He goes back to the door. Tim is standing at the door. He
leans down to the letter box.*

Help, help we need the Mayor, the townsfolk have
turned into sofas. Mr Mayor, Mr Mayor . . .?

The door opens. It's the Mayor.

(*looking at Knighty, then to the mayor*)

Oh bollocks. His room's at the back, you spazz.

KNIGHTY

How am I supposed to know where he sleeps?

MAYOR

What the hell is going on?

KNIGHTY

(*as he slides down the ladder*)

Leg it, lads.

MAYOR

Stop, thiefs! I know who you are . . . Criminals . . .
Scum . . .

*The Lads have run off. The Mayor slams the door shut. We
hear the ladder drop to the ground. He opens the door again,
looks around, sees the ladder and proceeds to take it into the
house.*

74 INT. FAGASH'S HOUSE – BEDROOM – DAY

*We cut upstairs to a close-up of Fagash as he wakes up in bed.
We pull away to reveal Darcy sat beside him. Darcy passes
him the soup. In this scene Darcy has no façade. He is totally
genuine.*

DARCY

You alright?

FAGASH

Yer . . . I'm just a bit, oh, ma head.

DARCY

Listen to me now, Wesley. There's some Lucozade there,
some grapes and a pen and paper. Nothing I say can do
anything, only you can help yourself, do you understand
that?

FAGASH

Er, yer a think so.

DARCY

Right, then use this time now to think. Don't worry
about the match, if you want to pull out, no problem,
I'm here for you, mate. If or when you need anything,
just call me.

*Darcy gets us and leaves, Fagash pours himself a Lucozade.
Even though Darcy has gone Fagash says thank you.*

75 INT. TIM'S HOUSE – KITCHEN – DAY

*Pat is sitting at the table; she has bruising around her cheek.
The kitchen is a mess. She sips tea, waiting for the toaster to
pop. Tim enters, sits down and drops his head. We can guess
what has happened.*

76 EXT. JO'S SHOP – DAY

*We see a shot of Jo's shop. Darcy pulls up in his Reliant Robin.
We see him secure it with his big chain. He then removes his
helmet and walks up to the door. The door is locked; we see
the closed sign. Darcy bangs on the door. We cut to a view of
Darcy from inside. He continues to bang. We see Jo go to the
door.*

DARCY
(*shouting through the glass divide*)
Are you on a break?

JO

I was watching *Neighbours* . . .

She opens the door.

> JO
>
> What happened to you the other night?

> DARCY
>
> It was an absolute nightmare. One of the Lads ended up in a right state. I stayed over at his place to make sure he was alright.

> JO
>
> Was he OK?

> DARCY
>
> I think he'll be alright. Did you get the cushions done?

> JO
>
> Yeah sure, they're upstairs.

> DARCY
>
> I'd better get them and shoot off. I need to get down to the club and get things sorted. I'm just starting to understand how the Lads are feeling. Are you coming to the fight tomorrow?

> JO
>
> I should think so. Are you nervous then?

> DARCY
>
> I am, as it's known in the trade, cacking my pants ever so slightly.

He motions to leave.

> I'll put you a ticket on the door then. I'm really sorry about the meal, Jo.

> JO
>
> It's OK, Alan, don't worry about it. I'll go and get them for ya.

Jo leaves to go upstairs, Darcy is left in the shop. He begins chatting away to an imaginary Jo, quietly laughing and joking with her in a way that he can't when she's there. This scene is quite humorous – the conversation one has with the mirror before going out on a date. Darcy stops and contemplates the fact that he knows he could never speak to her in this way. We stand in silence with him for a few seconds. It is an uncomfortable silence.

78 INT. BOXING CLUB – DAY

The day of the big match.

We are ringside with Darcy in the empty boxing club. It is early morning. He is sitting in contemplation. 'The Big Day' appears on the screen.

79 INT. TIM'S HOUSE – STAIRS – DAY

We cut to Tim's house and see him sneaking quietly down the stairs.

80 INT. FAGASH'S HOUSE – BEDROOM – DAY

We cut to Fagash sitting up in his bed contemplating smoking a spliff. He throws it in the bin and gets out of bed.

81 EXT. PARK – DAY

And finally we see the rest of the Lads sitting under their tree in the park. All look very nervous.

82 INT. BOXING CLUB – DAY

When we cut back to the club, it is just before the match starts. The cut happens on the sound of the 'ding, ding' of a ringside bell.

83 EXT. BOXING CLUB – ENTRANCE AREA – DAY

There is a carnival atmosphere. The local cadets are outside playing kazoos; the landlord from The Old Star is selling booze; flags and balloons are up and there is a crowd gathering.

84 INT. BOXING CLUB – DAY

The ring is spotless, surrounded by chairs. People begin to take their places.

Jim, the announcer, is testing the microphone – one two, two one – We see Ronnie sitting in the front row with Sharon by his side. We see Geoff sitting with the landlord from The Old Star; he's already pissed. Darcy is putting stools and buckets at opposite corners of the ring; we follow him from the ringside and see him go through a door, with the word 'Home' above it. Next to this is another door with 'Away' above. The scene cuts to the other side of the door marked 'Home'.

85 INT. BOXING CLUB – CHANGING ROOM – DAY

We see the Lads sitting in a dressing-room. On arrival there is silence. The Lads are in their kits. We hear a toilet flush and Fagash walks out.

FAGASH
We won't get dope-tested will we?

Nerves prevent anyone from replying. He walks forward a few steps and then turns and goes back into the toilet.

BENNY
Are you alright, Fagash?

Fagash nods.

The Lads are nervously shaking their legs and heads. All are seated, apart from Tim who is shadow-boxing.

Darcy enters.

95

DARCY

Sorry, everyone. Really sorry, I had a few things to see
to. Is everything OK?

KNIGHTY

Just about. Did you sort the music out with them,
Darcy?

DARCY

Yer we're havin' 'Achy Breaky Heart' and they're gonna
have 'Eye of the Tiger'.

BENNY

Achy Breaky Fuckin' Heart? You are jokin'?

DARCY

No.

GADGET

At least we got something to go in to.

BENNY
(*in disbelief*)
Achy Breaky Breaky Fuckin' Heart though!

DARCY
(*walking around the room*)
Come on then, Lads, heads up. You can do it, lads.
You've put the effort in, so just get out there and prove
yourselves. There's a lot of people who've come here just
to say told ya so.

*Fagash walks out of the toilet. He is sniffing badly; it's clear
that he's taken something.*

Fagash, you're first up, yeh, you ready?

Fagash turns and goes back into the toilet. Darcy smiles.

Just remember, you're in the same boat as them, they're
next door shittin' themselves, Lads, so don't worry,

alright? An' remember, when you get in the ring you are equal. Right? Right, Lads? Come on, right?

> LADS
> (*mumbling together*)

Yer, right, Darcy.

86 INT. BOXING CLUB – DAY

We cut to the away team. A band is playing. They are all well-built Lads. They're much more relaxed. We see them laughing and joking, and doing the occasional warm-up. We see their banner: 'STAFFORDSHIRE TERRIERS BOXERS – DEATH IN THE RING IS THE GREATEST HONOUR'.

87 INT. BOXING CLUB – CHANGING ROOM – DAY

We cut back to the Lads' changing room. Fagash comes out of the toilet again, this time he stays.

> DARCY

You about ready then, Fagash?

> FAGASH

No.

> DARCY

Good, right, lads. I'll see you out there. Stay calm and enjoy it.

One of the Lads throws a shoe at Darcy just as he walks out the door.

88 INT. BOXING CLUB – DAY

We cut back to the big hall. We see that nearly everyone has taken their seats. Geoff is still drinking with the landlord. Jo has arrived; she is standing at the back. Ronnie is smoking a massive cigar; his heavy-looking mates are smoking small ones in unison.

Standing by the side of the ring is Jim the announcer. Darcy is giving him instructions. Jim climbs into the ring, Darcy passes him the microphone and then runs to the tape machine. He gives Vernon (the Butcher) two tapes, then goes into the dressing room. Jim waits for the cadets to come in and the main doors to close.

JIM
Laaaddeezzzz aaaandaa Gentlemaannaa.

There are cheers and applause around the ring. We see Darcy smile.

Welcome welcome weeeellcomeee. Today's event is bought to you by Ronnnnnieee Marrsh Financesss.

We see a smiling Ronnie, who stands and waves to those behind.

And 101 Promotions. Featuring the yet unseen 101 Warriors against the Staffordshire Regiment Boxing Team. Each bout will be of four two-minute rounds, – three falls or a knockout will decide the winner. In the event of a bout going the distance then the referee's decision will be final. Arrreee we readayyy to rummmbleee?

More cheers and applause.

Introducing from the Staffs Regiment, weighing twelve stone . . . Phil 'The Animal' Yates.

Vernon starts the tape. The fighter comes through the door and into the ring accompanied by his trainer. Vernon fades the tape.

And now introducing the home town boy, also weighing twelve stone, it's Wesley Fagash Fraaaaseerr.

Vernon starts the tape. The door opens, Darcy walks out; he then goes back in and walks out, gently pulling Fagash by the

*arm. Fagash gets into the ring; Vernon fades the tape. Fagash
is clearly off his face. It takes a few moments for him to take
off his gown. His opponent looks much fitter and calmer.*

Roooound Oneaa.

*The bell rings for the start of the bout. The crowd cheer.
Fagash moves to the centre, he looks more like a boxer than
we would expect, ducking and weaving and moving around
the ring – the energy he is showing is due to the five grammes
of speed he had taken. His opponent hits him on the arm;
Fagash hits him back. This is the entire action of the round,
the bell rings, the crowd clap, a few boo.*

DARCY
(*sponging Fagash's face*)

You're blowing out in front of me, Wesley. Come on,
son, snap out of it.

Fagash's eyes are all over the place.

JIM

Roound Tooooaa.

*The bell rings. Both fighters start moving around. Fagash is
hit in the face, he stumbles back into a corner; his opponent
follows through and starts laying into him. Blood spurts out;
Fagash is taking blow after blow, forgetting to defend himself.
The gore is X-rated. Darcy throws in the towel. The winner
celebrates; Fagash puts his gloves up and moves around the
ring as if still fighting. Darcy grabs hold of him and takes him
to his corner. His face is badly cut up.*

DARCY

You're through it now, Wesley. You OK?

FAGASH

Fine, Mum.

He drops to the ground.

99

*We see separate shots of Darcy, Sally the Judge and Ronnie;
none is impressed. The scene moves on. In the ring is another
opponent.*

> JIM
>
> And introducing the home town boy Ian 'Wolfman'
> Knight.

*The music starts. Knighty and Darcy walk up to the ring.
From the back of the hall someone throws a piece of battered
fish which hits Knighty in the face.*

*Knighty is furious, he makes for the direction from which the
fish came; people clear their seats, Darcy grabs hold of him.
Order is restored. Knighty looks in good shape, the two boxers
look to be an even match.*

> Roound Onneaa.

*The bell rings for the first round. Both come out and
immediately exchange blows; they move around the ring well,
jabbing and diving. The round is clean, both fighters doing
well. We see shots of the crowd. Shouts of enthusiasm for both
sides. Knighty is hit with some good combinations towards the
end. The bell goes for the end of the round. There is nothing
to complain about this time.*

> DARCY
>
> Good one, mate. You need to get back at him when he
> behaves like that. You leave yourself too open.

> KNIGHTY
>
> Alright. Did you see me do the Ali Shuffle?

> DARCY
>
> No.

> KNIGHTY
>
> Oh, I'll do it again then.

DARCY

Don't bother.

JIM

Roounnda Toooaaa.

The bell rings and the Lads go at each other again. The boxing is quicker, more punches are thrown, more hits. Knighty is trapped against the ropes and covers up well against a vicious attack; he manages to grab his opponent and they are forced to break. The battle continues. Again Knighty is attacked; this time there are too many punches. He goes down, but only onto one knee. He shakes his head and gets up. The ref gives him the eight count. The fight continues, Knighty avoids any trouble and the bell rings.

DARCY

Ya doin' fine, son.

He sponges Knighty's face. There is a cut on his lip.

KNIGHTY

He keeps callin' me a puff.

DARCY

It's just ring banter, tell him you've slept with his mother.

JIM

Roounda Threeeeaa.

The bell rings. Knighty points at his opponent and shouts to the crowd: 'I've slept with his mother.' The crowd laugh and cheer. The boxing continues. We see a close-up of Knighty as he throws his punches. Punch 1: 'I've'. Punch 2: 'slept'. Punch 3: 'with'. Punch 4: 'your'. Punch 5: 'mother'. A close-up of the other boxer reveals him doing the same thing to: 'You are a fat puff.' We cut to an overhead view. The boxers are resting, just moving around the ring. The bell rings, the crowd applaud.

DARCY

Go on, son. Knock him over and you've done it.

JIM

Rooundaa Foooorrraa.

The two come to the middle. The opponent goes to touch gloves, Knighty whacks him. He hunts him down and lays punches into him. He falls to the ground. Knighty jumps in the air. The crowd boo his bad sportsmanship. His opponent can't get to his feet. The Ref helps the man up and raises his hand. Knighty can't believe it. He runs to the Ref and stands face to face with him.

REF

You're disqualified.

KNIGHTY

Fuck that.

He headbutts the Ref, who falls to the floor. He then pushes his opponent to the ground and starts kicking him. Darcy comes in and pulls him away; he still kicks out. The opponent's trainer is pushed back by Jim. There is booing in the crowd. A few people leave, including Knighty's parents. The cadets are ushered out. Ronnie doesn't look happy. Geoff has moved to ringside; he is shouting and cursing Darcy and his boxers. The Judge has decided to leave.

89 INT. BOXING CLUB – DRESSING-ROOM – DAY

The scene returns to the Lads' dressing-room. The Lads are listening to the noise. The door is flung open, Knighty is manhandled into the room by Darcy. Darcy pins Knighty against the wall, as he did in the earlier scene.

DARCY

Well.

We waits for a response.

KNIGHTY

Fuck off.

DARCY

What?

KNIGHTY

Fuck off.

DARCY

Get changed. You've no right to be wearing gloves.

KNIGHTY

What do you know? I beat him. You know it. You fuckin' know it.

DARCY

You lost. Who's hand did he raise?

KNIGHTY

I don't give a fuck. He was gone. He was gone, man.

DARCY

You lost control and you lost the fight. It makes me sick to see that sort of rubbish. You could have won that.

KNIGHTY

I did win it, Darcy. I won an' if you don't think I did then you can go to fuck.

DARCY

Just get changed.

Darcy goes out. The room is silent, Knighty is still furious.

YOUNGY

Lost then, did ya, Knighty?

90 INT. BOXING CLUB – DAY

Knighty throws his glove at Youngy. The Lads laugh. Order

has been restored, about half the crowd has left. The opponent has been introduced.

JIM

And now the local boy. Weighing eleven and a quarter stone, Tiiimmm Evans.

Tim walks into the ring with Darcy. Tim's Dad is pissed at ringside. The Mayor is seen standing in the doorway. Vernon fades the tape and goes to the ringside.

GEOFF
(*very drunk*)

You're a fuckin' idiot, son. Ya mother's at home in pain an' you're here tryin' to be some fuckin' boxer. Look at yourself, son. Ya mother hasn't been sleeping since you started doin' this – d'ya know Dad? D'ya remember me ah, son? Just 'cause am not some fat haggis who thinks he's fuckin' Micky Warren, don't mean ya fuckin' ignore me. Respect, son.

Geoff climbs into the ring, a deadly silence.

You, you, Alan Darcy. I know your game. I know your fuckin' game. You're just a fuckin' pimp. Which one you sleeping with now, ah? If you've bin near my lad I'll rip ya head off an' shit down it, d'ya get me? D'ya get me, ah?

The crowd is silent. We see Jo with her head in her hands. We see Ronnie, Sharon and Tonka leave.

DARCY

Come on, Geoff, let's sort this outside so the boy can fight.

GEOFF

No, fuck off. My boy's not fighting for you. He's coming home. Tim you're coming home. You're not fightin' any fucker for him. Are you listening to me, boy?

Darcy tries to get Geoff out of the ring.

Take your fuckin' hands off me, shit-face, or I'll knock you out, alright?

DARCY

Don't threaten me, Geoff.

GEOFF
(*very pissed*)
Why, what the fuck do you think you're gonna do, ah?

DARCY

Outside now, Geoff.

Darcy manhandles Geoff out of the ring; a passageway has cleared.

91 EXT. BOXING CLUB – DAY

As we follow them outside we see that a few fights have erupted within the building. The Mayor is outside already.

DARCY

Thanks for your support, I didn't think you'd show.

MAYOR

Going well, then.

GEOFF

You're fucked, Darcy.

DARCY

Geoff I'm warning you, just shut the fuck up.

As most of the spectators leave the area, a few gather around the ongoing argument, including all the Lads.

TIM

What's going on. Dad?

GEOFF

That's fuckin' right. son, I'm your dad.
(*to Darcy*)
You're just a piece of shit. You're the fuckin' laughing-stock.

He's prodding Darcy's chest.

Think you're some big man, don't ya? Think you can do the father shit, ah? Eighteen years, mate, eighteen years I've put into that fucker, an' you think you can come an take the boy away.

DARCY
(*grabbing Geoff's hand*)
He's not a fuckin' plant, Geoff. He's a grown man. Look at him. Take a look.

TIM

Fuckin' hell, the pair of ya.

DARCY
(*turning his attention back to Tim*)
Tim, listen to me. I've got space. Stay at ours. You can't live like this, son. He's messing up your life. I know. Just take the chance now, think of yourself for once.

TIM

Darcy, I'm goin' home. Mum's there, d'ya think I can leave her to get beat every day? I can't do it.

GEOFF

D'ya hear him? Now just fuck off an leave us alone. Sort your own life out, right? Sort ya own fuckin' life out. Everyone knows you're a fuckin' pervert. That's why you're doin' this.

DARCY

One more word, Geoff, and I swear.

GEOFF

What? What you gonna do, fuck-face?

KNIGHTY

It's not worth it, Darcy.

People are starting to gather round in a circle, others are simply leaving.

GEOFF

Tim's my son. I've seen ya tryin' to get him an' his mother away from me, don't think am blind. I've seen ya tryin' to pull us apart.

DARCY

Geoff, please.

GEOFF

When I get home tonight ya know what I'm gonna do? I'm gonna beat the pair of them senseless. Just so they remember.

Darcy cannot control his rage. For the first time we see him hit someone. He punches Geoff who drops to the floor like a sack of spuds. He sets about Geoff, throwing punches, kicking him and smashing his head against the floor.

DARCY

I'll fucking kill you, man, do you hear me?!

Darcy jumps up like a bolt and everyone shits themselves and moves out of his way. He looks wild. The Mayor stands silently at the side with a smug look on his face. He knows Darcy has blown it. Darcy begins to realise what he has done.

I'm sorry, Tim, I'm sorry, Tim.

TIM

(*to Darcy*)

What have you done, you stupid bastard?

Darcy goes to approach Tim.

DARCY

Tim?

TIM

Don't come near me, you fucking psycho.

DARCY

He was trying to ruin it for us, Tim.

Tim turns away and goes to help his Dad up. Darcy looks to the other Lads. They shy away from any eye contact. They are all dumbstruck by Darcy's act of violence. No one knows how to react or what to say. Jo walks off looking decidedly shocked. Darcy and everyone else knows the significance of this event. The club is finished.

(*desperately*)

Come on, Lads.

Dead silence. The odd thing about this scene is that no one dares make the first move to leave. It is painful to watch. The whole scene is powered along by what is not said. Darcy reads this as the Lads turning against him, when in reality they are merely unequipped to deal with the situation. Finally, it is the sound of a car pulling up that breaks the tension. Darcy turns around to see that a police car is arriving. The scene moves forward. We see an overhead shot of Darcy being put into the police car and driven away. The Mayor is driven away in his car. People scatter. The Lads stand and watch as Tim gets into the ambulance with his father. We fade to black.

92 INT. POLICE CELLS – DAY

Fagash is sitting in a police cell. There is a Guy next to him asleep. As Fagash finishes his fag the Guy wakes up.

> GUY

What you in for?

> FAGASH

I hit someone over the 'ead with a chair. They're gonna remand me this morning.

> GUY

What a nightmare . . . D'ya know what I'm in for?

> FAGASH

No, sorry, you were already here when I arrived.

> GUY

Right, oh well, it'll give us something to look forward to.

Fagash looks round at him baffled. The Guy offers him a fag, he takes one. They light up their cigarettes in synchronization.

93 EXT. BOXING CLUB – DAY

Apart from Tim and Fagash, all the Lads are at the gym. They are in front of the main doors, which have a lock and chain on them. There is a letter on the door, giving notice of renovation to build an indoor market.

> BENNY

Well, that's that, then.

> KNIGHTY

Not quite.

He steps back then kicks at the lock. The door bursts open.

I think we should pay our last respects to the ring.

94 INT. BOXING CLUB – DAY

Walk hand-held around the Lads as they pour lighter fluid onto a boxing glove and set it alight. The camera faces the Lads. The glove is thrown – 'whoosh' – the sound of the ring setting light is heard, as we slowly zoom in on one of the Lad's faces. We see the flames in his eyes. As we zoom further into the eye, all we can see is the reflection of the flames. As we zoom out the eye has become Darcy's.

95 INT. DARCY'S HOUSE – KITCHEN – DAY

The camera pulls away from the close-up eye with flames. We are with Darcy. He is sitting at the kitchen table. He is crying. There are two bottles of spirits on the table, one only half full, as well as two packed bags. Darcy holds a glass in his hand. After a few moments Darcy stands, puts on his coat, grabs the bags and leaves. 'Fallen Flower' by Gav Clark begins.

96 EXT. PARK – DAY

We cut to a shot of Knighty and co. at the park playing football.

97 EXT. TRAIN STATION – DAY

We cut back to Darcy as he walks away from the camera at the train station off into the distance.

> DARCY
> (*voice-over*)
> I felt for a moment that I was a prophet, but now I know I'm the fool.

98 INT. TIM'S FLAT – KITCHEN – DAY

FIVE YEARS ON.

The scene returns to the present. Tim is sitting at the table in

the kitchen, as he was at the beginning of the film. The ashtray has collected a small pile of cigarettes and the milk in his coffee has developed a layer of skin. He sits back with his feet on the table. He reads the final two lines or so of the diary before closing it.

He turns the book to look at the front cover. He seems to be on the verge of crying, the thoughts and confessions that he has just read have lead him to feel incredible pity and guilt for Darcy. The realization of his treatment towards Darcy has dawned on him during the course of reading.

It is clear to him that he is, in part, responsible for Darcy's departure from the town and his condition now.

The gentle hum of the washing-machine stops. The sudden silence evokes the isolation of this man, sitting in the kitchen with the victim of his past actions close to death in a bed above.

The camera tracks gently across the kitchen, the eerie silence continues . . . The camera comes to rest. Tim places the diary on the table and leaves the kitchen. The camera follows him up his stairs (hand-held) and into the bedroom.

99 INT. TIM'S HOUSE – BEDROOM – DAY

Darcy is still in the bed, propped up by pillows. The cut on his face has gone; the rough desert face is now clean and healthy.

At the end of his bed sits an Old Man; he appears to be a cross between God and Jesse from The Dukes of Hazzard. Darcy and the stranger are discussing Jake La Motta. The dog is nowhere to be seen. The Old Man is wearing a pair of old jeans, white plimsoles and a T-shirt.

The sense of time and reality within this scene is detached from real time. There is absolute dead silence. Moments of Tim moving in slow motion. Tim's eyes are transfixed as we cut between Darcy sitting up in bed talking to the stranger, then back to Darcy's body at rest. The Old Man is no longer there; it is not revealed whether Tim or only Darcy saw him. Still in silence, but back into real time, we see that Darcy has passed away.

Without any sound. we see Tim wipe his hand over Darcy's face, pulling his eyes closed. He takes Darcy's hand from his chest and places it by his side. The camera tracks back to a wide shot. The two are alone in the room . . . The silence is replaced by an angelic soloist who leads us into the next scene.

MONTAGE SEQUENCE

100 INT. TELEPHONE BOX – DAY

We see Tim making telephone calls to the Lads.

101 INT. KNIGHTY'S HOUSE – DAY

Tim visits Knighty.

102 INT. JO'S SHOP – DAY

Jo at her newsagent's. We have the impression that Tim has visited everyone who knew Darcy. The angelic music continues right to the end of Darcy's final speech, which runs throughout this sequence. We hear the final page from Darcy's diary – Darcy's final prophesy.

DARCY
(voice-over)
To give us the most splendid feeling. Letting go of your own for the pleasure of another.

Their last wish was to burn our church, with it they took my heart. As these are to be my last words, they should be brief.

If you hope, dream or wish, then you are undermining your present situation.

Be who you are.

Don't abuse things.

Understand yourself.

And give someone 5op when you see them sat alone wrapped in a blanket.

Alan Darcy, Autumn 1996

103 INT. CHURCH – DAY

DARCY'S FUNERAL

We see a close-up of Tim, at the front of the church, as the last two lines of Darcy's voice-over finishes. The camera tracks backwards, away from Tim, towards the back of the church. The church is empty.

We then hear the doors open and cut to a shot of the doors. We see people begin to turn up. The church begins to fill up with everyone who Tim has asked. We cut to a close-up of Tim. We see him smile.

The end credits will be in the form of long forward-tracking shots through the rows of pews showing the main characters and the performer's name. As each row stands and leaves, the camera tracks forwards to the next row, where the titles appear. This continues through each row. The song 'Monkey Dead' by Gavin Clarke begins and runs until its conclusion. We see all our main characters and are shown how they have changed in the five years since the boxing club. Knighty has a wife and kid. Daz is now Benny's boyfriend, etc. As the scene changes to the wake, where crew titles and rags are seen, the song 'Monkey Dead' concludes on this shot.

Credits

MAN OUTSIDE SHOP	John Baxter
KNIGHTY'S MUM	Maureen O'Grady
MAN WITH SAUCEPAND ON HEAD	Shane Meadows
MAN SELLING FLOWERS	Ben Rothwell
THE BOXING MATCH JUDGES	Ron Bissell, Mick Bleakley and Derek Osborne
STAFFORDSHIRE COACH	Derek Groombrisge
STAFFORDSHIRE BOXERS	Liam Walsh and Kevin Wallace
PHIL 'THE ANIMAL' YATES	Dave Miller
STEPHEN S. STEPHENSON JNR	Ginger Keane

CREW

1st Assistant Director	Gus Maclean
2nd Assistant Director	Gareth Williams
Production Co-ordinator	Winnie Wishart
Post Production Co-Ordinator	Lorraine Armstrong-Esther
Post Produciton Delivery Supervisor	Stephen Law Roger Brown
Script Supervisor	Cathy Doubleday
Script Editor	Robyn Slovo
Camera Operator	Ashley Rowe BSC
Focus Puller	Ian Clark
Clapper Loader	Richie Donnelly
Camera Grip	Devin D. Higgins
Camera Trainee	Edward Lee Wright
Sound Mixer	Rosie Straker
Dubbing Mixer	Pete Smith
Boom Operator	John Coates
Trainee Sound Assistant	Anstey Bligh
Unit Location Manager	Rob Jones
Location Assistants	Mick O'Reilly and Alison Pitman
Art Director	Niall Moroney
Assistant Art Director	Polly Richards
Art Department Assistant	Emma McDevitt
Production Buyers	Gillian Edwards and Astrid Sieben

Prop Master	Kenneth Augustin
Dressing Props	Brian Bird
Standby Props	Adam Southgate
Prop Runaround	Carl Jones
Chief Make-Up and Hair Designer	Pebbles
Make-Up and Hair Assistant	Tapio Salml
Additional Make-Up and Hair	Scott Beswick
Additional Make-Up and Hair Assistants	Adrian McKenzie, Suzanna Botterill and Melissa Walsh
Wardrobe Supervisor	Theresa Hughes
Wardrobe Assistant	David Sanderson
Additional Wardrobe Assistant	Tami French
Gaffer	John Donoghue
Best Boy	Bill Tracey
Electricians	David Wall and Paul Dibden
Assistant Editor	Coral Houtman
Sound Designer/Dubbing Editor	Simon Gershon
Dialogue Editor	Dave McGrath
ADR Recordist	Paul Harris
Foley Recordist and Foley Editor	Jeremy Price
Foley Artists	John Fewell and Julie Ankerson
Dubbing Assistant	Hugh Johnson
3rd Assistant Director	Ben Rothwell
Director's Assistant	Dominic Dillon
Production Secretary	Suzie Halewood
Production Accountants	Nigel Wood and Lita O'Sullivan of 101 Financial Consultancy
Accounts Assistant	Sara Dixon

WHERE'S THE MONEY RONNIE?

Shane Meadows

Where's the Money Ronnie?

After making ten or fifteen shorts (just for fun) with screenings among small audiences and friends, I decided to remake my first short and send it in to a few competitions. One thing I had learnt was to keep it simple, so I decided to base the whole thing around four opposing monologues delivered in a police interview room, leaving it to the audience to find out who was telling the truth. This film cost £250 to make, which was hugely expensive at the time, and became the calling card for both *Smalltime* and *TwentyFourSeven.* One of the actors, Mat Hand, turned up to do his section completely wired. He had been up all night in hospital with his newly born, ill son. He was going berserk in front of the camera to try to get it out of his system. I told him to do the same with his lines and set the camera running. Leaving the camera running became the basis of my working process.

Shane Meadows

RONNIE

I have this feeling that I have become the victim of a conspiracy.

BENNY

I wanted to get out. I needed to get out of that place! I needed to get away to the sunshine! I haven't seen the sunshine for months; the grey sky's coming down on my head . . . I needed to get out, to get out and do something, so Ronnie said do this robbery, and he forced me 'cos I wanted some cash and it all got a bit messy . . . I did it and I'm not proud of it really. I had to get the cash 'cos I had to do me home decorating, I need to get another Jasper Conran book to sort some things out . . . I've got some bad coving, and I needed to get it done! It was more than I could and I needed to get it done! And I needed the cash so I gave it to Jock, and Jock said he'd look after it and I said, OK, Jock, you look after it, and he looked after it! And then I saw him and he was being fucking followed by that idiot smug bastard! And I saw him and I had to get my cricket bat, I don't know why I took the cricket bat, but I took the cricket bat, and I saw him and he fucking went for him and the money! He was holding *my* cash! So I smacked him with my cricket bat! And it was hard! And then the car pulled up, and they were there, and they had cleavers and cricket bats and fucking everything, different items, scaffolding . . . and I thought we were gonna get killed! And Ronnie pulled a gun out and he shot them; he shot them twice! Once in the foot and once in the head . . . And I was quite scared and I was shouting, Where's the money, Ronnie? Where's the money, Ronnie? I don't know, I haven't got a clue, and it was very frantic and there was people everywhere fighting and sprawling and beating and vomiting, 'cos they'd been kicked in the guts so many times! And I didn't know what to do, I just wanted to lie on the floor but I had to lie on the floor 'cos I had a gun to my head! And I got really scared and I said, Where's the money, Ronnie? Where's the money, Ronnie? and they just flipped out and there was a foul scene in this market, and I just didn't want to be there . . . Oh man, it was horrible . . .

JOCK

No, it's nothing to do with me, I don't really know what you're talking about yet at all, you know. I was just minding my own business, you know, standing by the market and, hum, I seen Ronnie. I owed Ronnie some money, but no, anyway I already had some money on me you know, um, that Benny gave me for doing some cleaning work, like, round the house, some decorating and that . . . Benny gave it me last night and I still had it on me. Anyway, I see Ronnie coming over and I didn't know what to do, so I ran, he chased me. He scared me, you know, he really scared me, man . . . I just ran . . . Anyway, I ran and then he caught me. And took the lot, he took the whole £800 that I had . . . just at that point the Marzettis come down, I think there was three of them, with guns and everything, I've never been involved in any of that shit at all, you know, that's . . . really . . . I'm straight as a die . . . Anyway . . . involved with the Marzettis, I heard the bang first, of a gun, you know, somebody hit the deck, I don't know who it was; I seen Ronnie, he was still standing . . . You can take fingerprints if you like, you know, I was nothing to do with any of that at all, man, I've never held a gun in my life before you know, apart from at the fair . . . I mean, I don't know what to tell you, you know! I shouldn't be here at all, I havnae done anything wrong, I've been done injustice to, look at me, it's . . . and my money, man, I've been waiting for that money for a year you know! Me wife's gonna kill me, man! She'll kill me!

POLICE
You were involved in a card game this morning . . .

ZICO
We play cards every day, I mean, that's why I didn't mention it, nothing serious, passes the time, good for the mental arithmetic and alertness.

Do we have to go on? Well, we'd got out the car by then and even though there was five of us, you know what they say about, like, a mad person, how they have the strength of ten men? Well, this Ronnie and he was armed! He had guns, I think he had knives, and he was vicious! Well, that was only to protect the two men that seemed to be innocent. And because we thought we might have got hurt . . . It was a split second thing; we weren't out to cause violence . . . We were out for self preservation really, in case anything happened to us . . . You might hear one of the others say that I had a gun . . . but what I actually had was a starting gun that I had from when I wanted to be in the athletics team and that I couldn't because I was too fat 'cos of the pasta and that . . . And so I got the starting gun out and I just took that 'cos I thought if someone is gonna, you know, like attack us or anything, it might sort of make them think twice or thrice . . . and it just turned out for the worst really . . .

RONNIE
I suppose I would have done the same in the circumstances, but I'm trained, so I caught him up by the market, give 'im a bit of an 'iding, and said, you know, Where's the money? That's what I say, it's like my little punch-line, if you like . . . Even money collectors have to have jingles . . .

It looked to me like between one and two Gs, you know, two thousand pound. I immediately made the assumption that this might have something to do with this robbery . . . You know, where the fuck is Jock, of the Spoono, going to pull two Gs from all of a sudden? You know, and lo and behold, it's not fifteen minutes after the robbery! So I said, Listen, you gonna give me that money, you know, you're going to give it me. And he said, I ain't! You know, I'm not gonna give it you! It was like sort of a pantomime thing going on! Before I had a chance to forcefully take the money, I'd seen Benny Bould, just out of the corner of my eye, coming from round the back of one of these buildings – with a fucking cricket bat! And he wielded it a couple of times, caught me here, and as I went down from that smack – it was really quite gentle, but it made me dizzy – I banged my eye on the floor there, just a little nick . . . I got tunnel vision on, my main aim is: I'm trying to get the cash for the good of the people, I weren't going to get it for me, you know, I was getting it so that I could give it back! Thirty seconds after that a car pulls up with the Marzetti brothers in. There was Rico, Chico and Zico in this car and they were getting tooled up! There was a meat cleaver, a half a pool cue with the end drilled out, and Zico had a Magnum .45. I know in my heart that they were waiting for me in a conspiracy! The Marzetti brothers, even though they don't speak Italian, you know, they're from up North somewhere, they have got Italian roots, so I shot two! Yeah, I fucking killed two, and I don't feel bad about that 'cos they were coming at me, you know, it was going off . . . And I shot two people and I killed two people and I don't know what happened to Benny and his feet, but that's my story, and I'm sticking to that.

Credits

LEFT (SMALLTIME)

Shane Meadows

Smalltime

Smalltime came about on the realisation that after making twenty short films on Jubilee St in Nottingham people were pretty much all moving away fairly soon. I wanted us to celebrate what we'd done and make a longer piece, so I began writing *Left*. But time was not on our side so I very quickly wrote the basis for it; a group of smalltime crooks living on the left-hand side of the law. We shot thirteen hours of footage in nine days and produced a sixty-minute piece of improvised poverty to be renamed *Smalltime*. This was the film that took me to festivals all over the world. The band who formed to write the music became Sunhouse and got a five-album deal. Off the back of this and *Ronnie* I got the deal to write and direct my first feature, and the actors who had made all of these films so special would be able to come with me.

(I want to put the original screenplay of *Left* in place of the finished *Smalltime* script even though it's a bit pahoona, because it is the first thing I ever wrote.)

Shane Meadows

Note
Each scene is titled on screen with an underlayed still. The still will illustrate the theme of each scene.

Picture of Malcolm and his Wife outside a church.

Up a back alley in Sneinton a man is running with a sofa on his head which he dumps over someone's yard and runs off.

Hand-held. One shot. Two men are walking towards camera in a disused fruit market; the camera is moving back.

> JUMBO JOHNSON
> How can we get some wedge, man?

> MALCOLM POWDER
> I bet there's loads of lead on the roofs.

> JUMBO JOHNSON
> What are you fucking talking about? These are fruit fucking storehouses.

> MALCOLM POWDER
> No man, there's lead up there.

> JUMBO JOHNSON
> Lead?

Jumbo is taking the piss.

> MALCOLM POWDER
> Aye, lead.

> JUMBO JOHNSON
> Who told you that, man?

> MALCOLM POWDER
> Big Willy.

Jumbo starts to laugh.

> Fuck off, Jumbo.

JUMBO JOHNSON

I was talking to Bets the other day and he showed me all
the Buddha statues he's robbed; he's been trying to get
this big fucking white Buddha, man, but it's in a glass
case. He said if we tap it he'll give us half an ounce.

MALCOLM POWDER

No, man, I reckon the woman sussed me the other day. I
tell you what, though, that new pet shop's got loads of
fucking dog food standing outside in big crates, they
probably can't fit it in the shop. We could sell it to Big
Billy Black, man, he's got a couple of Staffies. We can
just wheel it up in shopping trolley.

JUMBO JOHNSON

What the fuck's going on in your head, Malc? Bets will
give us £50 for that statue, man. How are we supposed
to carry £50 worth of dog food. Let's just do the statue
shop. You don't have to do anything, man, just be a
decoy.

MALCOLM POWDER

I feel bad robbing from them, it's only a little shop.
Can't we rob the pet shop?

JUMBO JOHNSON

What are you talking about? It's a fucking chainstore,
they've got 'em all over the Midlands . . .

MALCOLM POWDER

They're a franchise business, they just buy the stock
from that company.

JUMBO JOHNSON

I don't give two fucks about these people. It's their
choice to open up a shop, it's their choice as to what
security they install. It's the game, man.

MALCOLM POWDER

Yeah, but they live up my street, the guy's got a disabled sticker on his car.

JUMBO JOHNSON

The guy's got a bad leg, what? That don't mean nothing to me, man, they say they want to be treated like normal people.

MALCOLM POWDER

That's where we differ, I ain't taking anything else from them.

JUMBO JOHNSON

I know what you're saying, man.

MALCOLM POWDER

Shall we try the pet shop, then?

JUMBO JOHNSON

Yeah, let's sweep up; that guy's a fucking nonce. I'll put one of those KKK cards under his door.

MALCOLM POWDER

He ain't a nonce, he just likes kids.

JUMBO JOHNSON

What is it with you? You never used to be a Jehovah's Witness.

MALCOLM POWDER

What is it with you? You never used to be a fuckin' Nazi.

Music comes in for opening titles.

JUMBO JOHNSON

Let' go rob the dog food.

Music is heard (Ram Raid Wreckers) as the last line is said.
Footage of our main characters: robberies, taking drugs,
fighting. The titles are held by the characters on screen. Each
character comes up to the lens with his title. When music ends,
cut straight back to the rest of Scene 1.

Jumbo and Malc are standing outside the back of a shop,
looking very suspicious. Malc is looking all over the place.
Jumbo is looking at Malc.

> JUMBO JOHNSON

What the fucking hell is wrong with you, man? You
look absolutely not one bit cool standing there looking
like you're about to assassinate the king. Chill out, it's
only a pet shop.

> MALCOLM POWDER

We're wide open here, I didn't realise how open it was.

> JUMBO JOHNSON

Shut the fuck up, Malc. No one'll say anything if we
look natural, they'll just think we're staff.

> MALCOLM POWDER

How many members of staff do you know who work in
this pet shop who transport stock in a shopping trolley
out of the stockroom and then wheel it up the high street
in completely the opposite direction to the shop's
shelves?

> JUMBO JOHNSON

Hold on just a minute, the way your conversation's
leading and the things that you're saying would give a
passerby the distinct impression that I was the one who
thought up this fuckarse plan. I wanted to rob – a –
that's one lightweight easy-to-carry Buddha statue from
a disabled shop-owner, and get exactly the same price if

not more cash for it than we will stealing and
transporting in the nightmare-mobile a very heavy and
highly embarrassing hundred tins of Chappie. So, shut
the fuck up, and climb over the wall.

Malc climbs over the wall but gets his jacket caught.

. . . Go on.

MALCOLM POWDER

I can't, my jacket's caught. Shit, man, Katy'll kill us if I
rip this, man. I've only had it a week. Jumbo, don't just
stand there, give us a hand.

*Jumbo climbs up and frees Malc. Malc carries on, Jumbo gets
back down. Malc calls out from the other side in a whisper.*

Jumbo, man, there's fucking loads of different types,
man. Which ones shall I get?

JUMBO JOHNSON

What is there?

MALCOLM POWDER

All the regular ones like Chum and that, a few cases of
Butcher's Tripe, Winalot Prime.

JUMBO JOHNSON

Get the Butcher's Tripe, Malc, that's about a pound a tin
in the shops.

MALCOLM POWDER

OK, but there's only two cases of that. Shall I get some
Chum?

JUMBO JOHNSON

We should stick to one brand, really. Are you sure
there's no more?

MALCOLM POWDER

Hold on, there's some smaller ones, called Butchers Mix.

JUMBO JOHNSON

No, man, they're not the same, they're bullshits of
Butchers Tripe, it's made by the same people that make
Chappie and Chunkie. You'll have to get a mix, did you
say there was some Prime?

MALCOLM POWDER

Aye, rabbit or chicken?

JUMBO JOHNSON

That'll do.

MALCOLM POWDER

Which one?

JUMBO JOHNSON

Both.

MALCOLM POWDER

What do you mean both? As in rabbit and chicken or as
in Butcher's Tripe and one of the flavours, or do you
mean both as in all three?

JUMBO JOHNSON

I mean both as in a mix of rabbit and chicken to add to
the Butcher's Tripe which we've already decided to take.

MALCOLM POWDER

I was just confused because you said you only wanted
one flavour.

JUMBO JOHNSON

I never said I wanted one flavour, I said I wanted one
brand if possible, I don't really care how many flavours
we get as long as we get a good brand.

MALCOLM POWDER

Got yer. Right here's the first case of Butcher's Tripe.

*The first case comes flying over the wall and nearly hits
Jumbo.*

JUMBO JOHNSON

Don't just throw it, you idiot. Pass it over, you nearly smashed my head in then.

MALCOLM POWDER

It'll take ages to keep climbing up and down.

JUMBO JOHNSON

You can't throw the Butcher's Tripe, it's too heavy to catch. I can hardly pick it up, never mind catch it.

MALCOLM POWDER

Exactly. You expect me to climb up and down a wall with it, though. I'll have to throw it.

JUMBO JOHNSON

If you throw it I won't catch it, which in turn will lead to the tins getting damaged, which will then make our chances of selling the goods a little slimmer, so I have no option but to revert to Plan Two.

MALCOLM POWDER

Go on . . . go on, what's Plan Two?

Jumbo opens the unlocked door and Malc is standing there . . .

You bastard.

Both men burst out laughing and then start to load up the trolley with the dog food.

JUMBO JOHNSON

I think we're going to have problems steering this shopping trolley, Malc.

MALCOLM POWDER

No worries, man. I checked about ten of them out down at Kwik Save, this one's a dancer, man, dead straight, no wobble.

Cut to the two men in the middle of the high street. The trolley has tipped over and the contents are on the floor.

Cut: backstreet, the trolley wheel is stuck in a drain.

Cut: backstreet, it won't steer properly.

Cut: arguing over who's turn it is.

Cut: they arrive at the guy's house, steer trolley down his path, knock on door. Billy Black answers the door.

> BILLY BLACK
>
> Alright, boys, you look fucked.

> MALCOLM POWDER
>
> We've just pushed this lot up from town.

> BILLY BLACK
>
> What is it?

> JUMBO JOHNSON
>
> Cheap dog food, Bill. We thought you might want it for your Staffies.

> BILLY BLACK
>
> Nice one, how much have you got?

> JUMBO JOHNSON
>
> Two cases of Butcher's Tripe.

> BILLY BLACK
>
> They won't eat that, it's too rich.

> MALCOLM POWDER
>
> You're joking, aren't you? This is a quid a tin.

> BILLY BLACK
>
> Dogs don't understand that, Malc. What other brands have you got?

> MALCOLM POWDER
>
> Winalot Prime.

BILLY BLACK

Have you not got any Chappie?

JUMBO JOHNSON

No, that's it.

BILLY BLACK

Sorry, lads, they won't eat any of those.

MALCOLM POWDER

They would if they were hungry enough.

BILLY BLACK

I'm not gonna starve my dogs just to save a few quid.
You should of give us a call before you got it, I would've
told you what to get. If you'd got Butcher's Mix, I'd
take it all off your hands right now.

MALCOLM POWDER

I don't fucking believe this, that's fucking you, that is,
Jumbo. I tried to fuckin' get some Butcher's Mix.

JUMBO JOHNSON

I wasn't to know, was I, you dumb prick? What the fuck
are we gonna do with this lot . . . Can we leave it here,
Billy?

MALCOLM POWDER

We're not leaving it after all that, Jumbo, no way.

BILLY BLACK

You can't leave it here, lads, you've only just pinched it.
I don't want it in my front garden.

JUMBO JOHNSON

I'm not taking it home, Malc. If you want it, you can
have it.

MALCOLM POWDER

Thanks a fucking million, I'll just push it all the way
home then, by myself, see you later, Billy.

138

BILLY BLACK

See you, Malc . . . Do you fancy a smoke, Jumbo?

JUMBO JOHNSON

Nice one.

MALCOLM POWDER

Fuck you, you pair of bastards, just wait till I've sold it all, Jumbo. I'll not give you a penny out of it.

Malc heads off up the drive. Jumbo and Billy are in hysterics.

2 MEN, WOMEN, CHILDREN

Portrait of Malcolm, Kate and the Baby.

In all the main characters' home environments: colour. Shot as a series of photographs; no camera movements. We cut between each house as the same argument happens; all the lads are going out for the afternoon, and all the girls are staying in.

MALCOLM POWDER

Do you think there's any difference between dog and cat food?

KATE LEMON
(*laughing*)

What?

MALCOLM POWDER

Big Billy Black give us a crate of dog food for the cat.

KATE LEMON

Why dog food? If we had a dog you'd come back with cat food.

MALCOLM POWDER

Aye, I know, I'm sick of being a fucking tea-leaf, Kate. Everytime I do anything I feel fucking dirty.

KATE LEMON

Do you think Jesus is playing a part in your life?

She bursts out laughing.

MALCOLM POWDER

Fuck off, I'm being serious. I've had enough of being a fuckin' tea-leaf, I don't want to be inside now we got the wee-un.

KATE LEMON
(*laughing*)

I'm sorry, do you want some crispy pancakes . . . McVicar.

She bursts out laughing as she walks into the kitchen. She calls from the kitchen.

Shall we take Gabe to Skegness?

MALCOLM POWDER

Aye, that'd be great, I really need a break from the lads. We get a Giro tomorrow – we can shoot up this weekend if you like.

KATE LEMON

How much do you owe out this week?

MALCOLM POWDER

I only owe Bets that fiver for the weed, and Jumbo's subbing me for tonight.

KATE LEMON

How much is that gonna cost?

MALCOLM POWDER

I don't know, it's not gonna be a mad one, though. I'll be back by ten-thirty.

KATE LEMON

Just fuck off, you liar.

MALCOLM POWDER

I will, I promise . . . Did you iron my shirt?

KATE LEMON

Who the fuck do you think I am, Kate slave fool?

MALCOLM POWDER

For fuck's sake, I can't iron, I get cash and pay the bills.

KATE LEMON

Don't give me that, this is exactly what I mean, you take me for a fool.

MALCOLM POWDER

What does that mean?

KATE LEMON

The fucking dog food sitting there, and don't insult my intelligence by trying to cover it up, because I saw you pushing it up the high street.

MALCOLM POWDER

I do it for you! How else can I make money! What's happened to you, Kate, you've always known what I'm like.

KATE LEMON

Yes, but over the years I've seen the numerous stupid things you get up to, everything you touch turns to double glazing.

MALCOLM POWDER

You know I'm trying to change, Kate, it's just the lads, they give me loads of shit about how I am with you and that.

KATE LEMON

Stand up for yourself.

MALCOLM POWDER

I will . . . Can you iron my shirt?

Right that's it, I'm going to my mum's. I don't have to put up with this.

MALCOLM POWDER

Good, I'll stay at Jumbo's tonight . . . God almighty, I don't know what's wrong with you, if you think you get it bad here, you should try living with Jumbo.

Kate ignores Malc so he puts on his coat and heads for the door.

See you later, my Angel, do you want some ox crisps and Pepsi bringing back . . .? Oh, fuck off, Mrs Mardy Poo Pie Shitty Dirty Mardy Fucking Shitarse.

Malc leaves the house. As he walks out the back door he finds the sofa chair that was dumped there.

Who the fuck's dumped this shit in my garden? Katy have you seen this fucking great chair out there? Some cunt's dumped it here, Katie . . .? Katie! Oh fuck it.

Malc kicks the chair but falls over it, loses his rag and walks off down the alley-way.

In Jumbo and Ruby's flat: Jumbo is waiting for Ruby to make his tea and iron his shirt.

JUMBO

Where's my tea . . .? Oi, where's my tea, Rube, you fucking halfwit?

RUBY

Watch your mouth, man, I'll stick a fucking knife in your heart if you don't shut it, do you get me?

JUMBO

Come here, you disobedient fucking animal!

RUBY

One more word, go on, one more word and I swear on
my life I'll fucking knife you, you evil bastard.

JUMBO

Oh God, look at the time, where's my shirt, you fucking
slapper? You're useless. Get you and your fucking accent
and your fucking shit and get out of this flat . . . I'm not
joking, get out . . . I mean it.

*Ruby can be heard shuffling about in a drawer; she pulls out a
carving knife.*

RUBY

You're dead, I'm gonna cut you up.

*Jumbo laughs and she tries to stab him; he moves and she
stabs the sofa.*

JUMBO

Look at that hole, what did you do that for? My mum's
still paying for that, you've stabbed the sofa, look at it,
you fucking dickhead? Give me that knife now.

Jumbo goes for the knife, Ruby cuts his hand.

Ow, you've cut me, it really stings, you idiot! Put that
fucking knife down . . . now!

RUBY

Get back, man, you know I'll do it.

JUMBO

I'm not gonna hurt you, just give me the knife.

RUBY

Who do you think I am? You're gonna leather me the
minute I put this knife down.

JUMBO

Don't be daft, I can't iron can I? I want to make a truce,

I ain't gonna smack you, am I? You'll probably poison me, just put the knife down and give us a kiss.

RUBY

OK, but if you lay one finger on me, I swear I'll have revenge.

JUMBO

I know, that don't I? Come here now, love.

RUBY

I'll put the knife down, but you can forget that romantic shit.

JUMBO

What do you mean?

RUBY

I can read you like a book. You've got a hard-on, right, and you want a quick ride before you go out, well you can fuck off!

JUMBO

You bastard, I don't have to listen to this, give me that fucking knife.

She goes to stab him again.

When you put that down I'm gonna smash your fucking teeth out.

RUBY

Well I ain't gonna put it down them am I, you dumb mother-fucker?

JUMBO

What about when you go to bed?

RUBY

I've got some whizz to keep me up, I'll wait for you to fall to sleep and I'll put this in your belly.

JUMBO

You're nothing but a loud foul-mouthed slapper, look at my sofa! My mum got me that, she's still paying for it, I feel really bad about it, she's skint. Why did you have to do that?

RUBY

I'm sorry, I wish you would just lay off me a bit, you're sending me mad, just chill out a bit, Jumbo, I'm not a slave.

JUMBO

You know I don't mean it.

RUBY

I know, I enjoy arguing with you – I don't want some soppy bastard, it's just that you get a bit over the top sometimes.

JUMBO

I'm not the one with the knife in my hand.

Ruby puts the knife down. Jumbo punches her in the face, and sets about giving her a good beating. We cut outside and the Lads are there. They can hear Jumbo hitting Ruby. Malc knocks on the door. Jumbo comes to the door.

MALC

What's going on in there?

JUMBO

I'm giving her a good hiding, that's what.

MALC

Leave it out, man, you don't have to fucking hit her.

JUMBO

For a start, it's got absolutely nothing to do with you, and, secondly, she's tried to kill me –

(*holding up his hand*)
– and she's stabbed my new sofa.

CRUTCH
Your mum's still paying for that, isn't she?

JUMBO
I know that, don't I?

CRUTCH
You can swap it for a new one, they'll take it back if it's
the first six months.

JUMBO
With a knife wound?

CRUTCH
You can fray the edges and make it look like a
manufacturer's fault.

JUMBO
I never thought of that . . . Ruby are you alright?

*All the Lads burst out laughing. Ruby starts to get up. Jumbo
and the Lads walk off. We cut inside to Ruby as she is
recovering. She walks into the bathroom, gets some razor
blades and bleach, goes into the bedroom, looks directly into
the camera.*

RUBY
I'm going back to my mum's, but first I'm going to put
these razor blades and this bleach in the bed. He'll get
into bed pissed out of his head, fall asleep and hopefully
lacerate his main vein.

*She pulls the sheets back, pours bleach over his side of the bed
and puts the razor blades in.*

3 AN AFTERNOON WITH THE LADS

Photo of all the Lads looking very eighties.

147

Music (Teenage Propaganda) fires up for Scene 3, a musical sequence with the Lads going round to Bets' flat, smoking bongs, getting loads of munchies, playing Nintendo, intercut with Kate Lemon with the kids at home cleaning, and Ruby doing a whole array of evil things around the house.

Fly on the wall-style. Bets' flat. Ricky, Jumbo, Bets and about five other Lads are in the front room. They are really stoned. The conversation seems aggressive, but this is the way they always speak to each other. They are playing or waiting for their turn on the Nintendo.

MALCOLM POWDER

Who's got my lighter?

JUMBO JOHNSON

He's off again with his fuckin' lighter. What are you, a fucking spastic? You never even had a lighter.

MALCOLM POWDER

Where's Bets? He had it last, oh man, I bet he's gone to put it in that fuckin' drawer with all the others he's fuckin' tapped off me.

GENIE

Jumbo have you got my fuckin' chomp bar, you slimy bastard? I wondered why you took my fuckin' coat.

JUMBO JOHNSON

I've eaten it, you shouldn't be such a fuckin' tool. I mean, man, if someone offered to take my coat when they knew I had chocolate in the pocket, I'd know exactly what was going on. I've done you a favour, man, next time it might be something of greater value than ten pence and you'll remember this experience.

Bets walks into the room.

BETS

You're not gonna take that are you, Genie? If he tapped

my chocolate, I'd squirt washing-up liquid in his eyes.
Have you got a light, Malc?

Everybody bursts out laughing.

> MALCOLM POWDER
> Fuck you, bastard, I only bought that lighter two hours
> ago. If I ever find your stash, man, I'll put a fuckin'
> bomb in it.

> CRUTCH
> Bets man, this ain't a Müller Fruit Corner, it's a fuckin'
> bullshit, you got me the wrong one, man, this ain't a
> Müller.

> BETS
> I know, I needed ten pence for some skins.

> CRUTCH
> Man, I'd have given you ten pence, I don't want this shit.

> JUMBO JOHNSON
> Give it here, you stupid bastard . . . Thanks, it's made by
> the same people who make the Müller yoghurts, man,
> it's exactly the same.

> BETS
> Have you got that lighter, Malcey?

*Everybody bursts out laughing, including Malc. Camera cuts
to outside Bets' door. The door opens and they all walk out.*

*In this scene they all walk and talk down the steps of the flat.
This is all going to be filmed in one shot. They go all the way
down the stairs, and when they get to the bottom they realise
that what they went to the flat for is still up there, and they
argue about who should go back up to fetch it. In the end
they all go back up and back down again. One shot of
between seven and ten minutes.*

This whole section is improvised until the second time they

149

*come down the stairs when they sing the famous opera song
'Figaro' all the way down the stairs, building to a crescendo.
Starts with Malc; ends with everybody singing.*

MALCOLM POWDER

La, la, la, lar, la, la, la, la, lar, la, Figaro, Figaro, Figaro,
Figaro, Figaro, Figarooooooo . . .

*Etc. Malc's voice can be heard over the others talking. They
all join in after about thirty seconds.*

EVERYBODY

Figarooooooooo . . . La la la laaa la, la la la laaaa la, la la la
la la la la la la la la la la, Figaro, Figaro, Figaro, Figaro,
Figaro, Figaro, Figarooooooooooooooooooooooooooooooooo.

*They continue all the way down the steps until they reach the
bottom, at which point they are screaming the song.*

*This section is to be worked on. The Lads drinking, playing
pool, wrestling and playing cards. Malcolm walks home pissed.
He closes the door and the music stops.*

4 JOCK'S CAFÉ

Picture of the café, with title in window.

*For the dance scene many different visual styles are
incorporated. Each café character has their own way of being
filmed, i.e. the Waitress will be filmed in colour on a trolley,
going round the café serving people.*

*Black and white, fly on the wall. Malcolm's house. The phone
is ringing. Malcolm answers the phone. Wipe to telephone
conversation, half screen for each person.*

JUMBO JOHNSON

Malcolm?

MALCOLM POWDER

Aye.

JUMBO JOHNSON

It's Jumbo, are you coming to Jock's?

MALCOLM POWDER

Can you sort us a sausage sandwich? I'm broke.

JUMBO JOHNSON

You can sub a deep-sea diver. I've got something lined up, man, it's cool.

MALCOLM POWDER

Nice one, I'll see you in about half an hour.

JUMBO JOHNSON

Half an hour? You only live round the fucking corner.

MALCOLM POWDER

I'm watching *Vintage EastEnders*.

JUMBO JOHNSON

What the fuck are you talking about, soap beast?

MALCOLM POWDER

It started about a month ago, it's all the old episodes, man, every morning, Dr Leg's in every episode, and Dirty Den and everyone. Pauline Fowler looks like a different person. It's on before *Anne and Nick* every morning.

JUMBO JOHNSON

Vintage EastEnders?

MALCOLM POWDER

Aye.

JUMBO JOHNSON

Oh nice one, man, is Mary in it yet?

MALCOLM POWDER

Aye, Dr Leg's helping her get a new place to live.

JUMBO JOHNSON

I remember that one. Oh, nice one, is it on every
morning?

MALCOLM POWDER

Yeah, man, Monday to Friday, me and Kate have taped
every one so far.

JUMBO JOHNSON

Cool, that's really fucking cool, man, do you fancy
watching some this afternoon?

MALCOLM POWDER

Aye, I'll bring the tapes with me, we can watch them at
Bets'.

JUMBO JOHNSON

Nice one, I'll score some weed.

MALCOLM POWDER

Nice one, Jumbo, I'll see you in about half an hour.

Both men put down their phone.

*Cut to outside Malc's house. Jazzy music – a Man is running
up the side of his house and dumping rubbish on Malc's back
yard. The Man runs off. Cut back inside to Malc's house. He is
just getting ready to leave. Leaves house and sees the rubbish.*

MALCOLM POWDER

What the fuck's this?

He looks around.

I'll fucking kill him.

He throws it back over his wall and walks off. Cut.

*Black and white: inside Jock's café with Jumbo, Bets, Crutch,
Genie and Dude. They are all talking about a post office job.
Everyone else in the café is frozen still. The only sound is a
distant radio and the dialect of the Lads on the table.*

BETS

Not one of us has any history of armed robbery, right?
So as long as the job doesn't turn into a farce, we ain't
gonna be the immediate suspects. Do you know what
I'm saying? We've got reputations, but it's only the
rogue factor. We're the ones they expect to pinch the
fucking Christmas tree, or set bonfires alight the night
before. If we make this job look a hundred per cent
professional, we're the last place they're gonna look. If
they do pinch us, it won't be as suspects, it will just be
procedure, in the hope that we know something.

DUDE

Listen, Bets, I'm up for it and that, but I ain't taking a
real gun, you can get life for that. If we're gonna use
guns, we might as well rob a fucking merchant bank,
we'd still get the same sentence.

BETS

We're gonna use fake gas and a couple of replicas, if they
suss us, we can just fuck off. That's the magic of robbing
a small place, the security is wank. They can't lock us in.
We can't lose.

CRUTCH

Everybody that ever planned a fucking job says that,
Bets. We've got to think everything over, man.

JUMBO JOHNSON

Listen, Crutch, you ain't even got to do fuck all, you're
the look-out, two years, top whack, so don't talk about
thinking things through, I ain't gonna risk a ten stretch
on some fucking whim. Me and Bets have got this sussed,
man. Bets is gonna do all the talking in a scouse accent,
and these fake gas canisters let off one burst of CS gas. So
we can blast some sucker in the queue with that,
everyone will shit it. I hope that filthy slag of mine's in
there, man, I'll shoot her straight in the fucking eyes.

Everyone laughs: Malcolm enters and pulls up a seat.

MALCOLM POWDER

Alright, lads, what's funny?

Everyone says hello.

Can you sort us that Bluey, Jumbo?

JUMBO JOHNSON

Yeah, man, here's a tenner, just give us one back on your
Giro.

MALCOLM POWDER

Oh nice one, Jumbo, I really appreciate it, man, I'm
absolutely broke.

DUDE

You couldn't sub us a fiver as well, could you, Jumbo?

JUMBO JOHNSON

You ain't paid me back for that sixteenth yet.

DUDE

I told you I can't give you that till Wednesday.

JUMBO JOHNSON

That's not my fault, is it, you prick? You know the score
at the Bank of Jumbo, 'one debt at a time', so my clients
don't get in over their heads.

DUDE

Forget it, Jumb.

JUMBO JOHNSON

Don't get shirty with me, you little turd.

MALCOLM POWDER

It's alright, Dude, I'll sub you couple of quid out of this.

JUMBO JOHNSON

No you won't, I just fucking gave you that. If you lend

him any, you breach your contract with the Bank of Jumbo, and I'll have to enforce my high interest policy on you with a vengeance so full of wrath you raise cash and build a college in my name.

Malcolm looks blankly at Jumbo for a few seconds then gives the money to Dude.

What a fat tosser, man, that's the last time I let you near the cash counter, you Scotch egg.

CRUTCH
Are you gonna ask him then, Bets?

BETS
Yeah, listen, Malc, we weren't gonna ask you, but we've got a job coming up and ain't got a driver.

MM
Don't, man, I don't even want to know, I can't risk anything now I've got the lad and that.

GENIE
Just let him tell you, you know me, Malc, I wouldn't touch anything big, but this is fucking classic. Serious, man, it's like a dream.

DUDE
Don't, lads, if he don't want to know then leave it, he's got a kid, I wouldn't do it if I had a kid.

JUMBO JOHNSON
What are you talking about, Dude? The driver gets fuck all, man. You'd have got worse if they'd pinched you with that ounce of whizz. Malc, if everything goes wrong, you're looking at twelve months tops. You've been going to counselling with your missus, they'll give you a social report, man, you'll probably walk out with a fucking arts grant.

BETS

Just listen to the plan, Malc, if by the end of it you ain't
begging to drive that car, I'll give you slight chafing
around the left shoulder-blade.

MALCOLM POWDER

OK, you bastards, hit me with what you got.

*Cut. The radio begins to crackle as though someone is tuning
in to a different station. We cut to a hand on the radio which
tunes in the song to which the dance will take place. The café
characters come to life and the dance of the Lorry Drivers
begins. The Lorry Drivers are filmed in colour in wide shots.
Macro of Jock the chef in black and white documentary, in his
kitchen. The Old Couple are filmed in a photograph style;
they never move. The Waitress is in exaggerated colour on a
trolley serving everyone in the café. (They will all be
incorporated into the dance.) While the dance sequence
happens the Lads are all totally frozen. When the music ends
everyone in the café freezes and we cut back to the lads' table.*

JUMBO

What do you think? Isn't that just the sweetest fucking
plan that could ever have graced Jock's splendid little
eating parlour?

MALCOLM POWDER

Shit, I'm fucked, you got me, you bastards, you got me.
I'm away with Kate at the weekend so I'll not see you
till Sunday.

BETS

Nice one, Malc, have a nice time, man. Don't even think
about this, we've thought of everything for you.

*Everyone says goodbye and Malcolm leaves. Just as the door
closes we cut into music and the opening of Scene 5.*

Advert picture of a hot dog.

Malcolm and Kate are at home packing. They're about to leave for Skegness. We cut to outside their house as the Man from before runs up and dumps a Hoover in Malc's garden. Malcolm and Kate walk out of the door after he's run away, and see the Hoover.

KATE LEMON
What the fuck did you bring that Hoover back for?

MALCOLM POWDER
I never brought it, some bastard's dumped it there. I found an old fucking sofa chair there the other day and then a big bag of shit yesterday.

KATE LEMON
Have you upset somebody?

MALCOLM POWDER
I'll do more than upset them when I find out who's doing it. It's probably that old cunt at the end, I'll chin him if I find out it's him, I don't care how old he is.

KATE LEMON
Shut up, let's go. We can sort it out when we get back.

They walk over to the door and pick up their bags and a box of rubbish comes over the wall.

MALCOLM POWDER
Right, you bastard, you're a fucking dead man.

Malcolm starts to chase the man round the back alley. They both run off down the road. Malcolm catches up with him and starts to threaten him.

MALCOLM POWDER
What the fuck did you dump the shit in my garden for?

HOT DOG MAN
You wouldn't let my lad play with your lad, would you?

MALCOLM POWDER
Oh, that was your fucking lad, was it? My lad's only nine months old, your lad's about ten.

HOT DOG MAN
He's only eight.

MALCOLM POWDER
He was trying to give my lad toffee.

HOT DOG MAN
You wouldn't let your lad play with my lad, though, would you?

MALCOLM POWDER
What did you dump a Hoover in my garden for?

HOT DOG MAN
Do you want some of that?

MALCOLM POWDER
Ha! Ha! I'll fucking brain you!

HOT DOG MAN
Go on then . . . Don't, please don't!

Malcolm thumps the Man once in the face, the Man falls over like a sack of spuds. Malcolm walks off.

I'll have the fucking pigs on you, that's fucking assault, that is!

Cut to inside Kate's car, with Malc and baby. They're on their way to Skegness, having a laugh.

KATE LEMON
Did you really smack him hard?

MALCOLM POWDER

I hardly touched him, he went straight down like a
fucking lead balloon.

KATE LEMON

What on earth was he thinking about, man? He was
totally off his head, I mean, dumping a Hoover over
someone's garden 'cause you wouldn't let their kids stuff
toffee down a baby's throat.

MALCOLM POWDER

Just wait till we get back, I'll have two tons of quick-set
concrete dropped in his garden.

KATE LEMON

We're here, look, there's the sea. I'm really glad we've
got Gabe with us, even though he won't remember it, it's
still really nice coming away as a family.

MALCOLM POWDER

Aye, nice one, we'll buy one of those disposable cameras,
take some pictures for him to look at when he's older.

KATE LEMON

You're gonna be a great dad.

*Cut to Skegness, music section, very photographic. Lots of
camera clicking. We follow our three characters around
Skegness for the day, eating candy floss, in the sea, on the
beach, up the sea front. A couple of minutes of family in the
sun to music and then we start to fade up their dialogue as
they're talking to the owner of a hot dog van.*

HOT DOG MAN

On an average season day I still pull a thousand quid, no
trouble.

KATE LEMON

You're joking, aren't you?

HOT DOG MAN

I'm deadly serious, and it's ninety-nine per cent profit.
You know yourself you can buy ten hot dogs in the
shops for about thirty pence. I can get a hundred for that
price, wholesale. The most expensive thing to buy is the
bread.

MALCOLM POWDER

So why are you selling it then?

KATE LEMON

Malcolm!

HOT DOG MAN

No, it's alright, it sounds strange, doesn't it? But you can
see yourself, I'm no spring chicken. Me and the wife
have decided to move to Greece. She's got a bad knee
joint, and this climate doesn't help, so we're set on
somewhere hotter, I just need to sell this place and
transfer me savings.

MALCOLM POWDER

Fairplay to you.

KATE LEMON

When do you need to sell up by?

HOT DOG MAN

Before the season starts really, we've had an offer from a
local chip shop, but I'd rather sell it to someone like
yourselves.

MALCOLM POWDER

I'm sorry, big man, it's not really my scene, thanks for
the offer anyway.

HOT DOG MAN

Just think about it, I don't expect you to decide just like
that, take our number and give us a call in couple of
weeks.

KATE LEMON

Thanks very much, I'll see if I can talk him round.

HOT DOG MAN

Well, take care of yourselves now, and give us a call about the van, it'll be nice if I can sell it to someone like yourselves.

MALCOM POWDER

Alright, mate, we'll call you either way, but don't hold on if you get an offer.

They all part. Cut into car on the way back home. Kate and Gabe are asleep. Malc is driving the car and it is very peaceful. He is deep in thought.

6 THE CROOK, THE GEEK, HIS MISSUS AND HER BROTHER

Picture of all the key characters from this scene.

The opening consists of a soundtrack which is overlaid with our robbers' preparation for the robbery. Each character is at home, talking to himself in disguise in his mirror.

MALCOLM
(holding a big pole)

OK, fuckers, get down! Who said that . . .? Right, come here, fucker . . . Wham! that's what happens to the next fucker who I hear even fucking breathing. Do get that, I mean business. I want something to go wrong 'cause I'm a fucking raving schizo, try me, fuckers, try me.

JUMBO
(with gun)

Lick it, lick it, yahoo, I want to kill everybody, you all mean nothing to me you, fuck-wipes, you're not going to be alright, I'm gonna kill you all before I start because I don't trust anybody, bang, bang, bang, bang. You, I need you to open the safe, move.

BETS
(*with a gas canister*)
I am the Ninja Lord Fuck Sword, I am trained to kill, I
kill when people look at me or when I need to piss or
shit, or eat or fucking anything.

DUDE
(*arguing and fighting with the bed*)
Are you looking at me, you? Whack, whack, whack.

He dives on the bed, fights it, gets up, looks in the mirror.

Are you looking at me? I didn't think so.

GENIE
(*runs in the room to try out his opening line three times*)
Everybody down, down on the ground, down on the
ground without a sound . . . Nobody move or
somebody gets it, oh shit, what am I gonna say . . .?
Right I've got a gun, you haven't, so be very careful not
to get on my tits . . . Cool, that's the one.

*Soundtrack continues as they all make their way to Jock's
café, trying out their various robbery techniques. They all
meet outside; Malcolm arrives in his own car.*

BETS
Is this a joke?

MALC
What?

BETS
The Metro.

MALC
No, we'll put Crutch and Dude in the back.

Everybody looks fucked off and starts huffing and puffing.

163

BETS

Where's the van?

MALC

The Guy caught me robbing it, I had to fuck off.

JUMBO

We gave you the money to hire one, you bastard. What happened to that?

MALC

I've spent it.

BETS

Right, I'm gonna do you.

Bets lunges for Malc. Malc drives forty yards up the road and leans out of the car.

MALC

It's OK, I'll park it round the corner.

BETS

Everybody round here knows the Ginger Minge Metro, and you expect us to rob our local post office in it?

JUMBO

I can't believe this, that shit-heap only goes fifty with one person in it, never mind six people. Trying to escape at high speed. If we get caught in that the pigs will have a field day.

MALC

It's all we've got.

DUDE

Bets, we can't rob it in that.

BETS

We'll have to – we'll park it down the end of the alley.

[*Final scene to be worked on*]

Smalltime Afterword

I wrote *Left* in my dinner hour on a daily basis whilst working as a volunteer at Intermedia Film and Video in Nottingham. Never having written a script before, I was simply going to use this material as a basis for improvisation and a backbone structure to ensure that the film wasn't a sloppy lump of shite that ran on for fourteen hours.

I enjoyed the process of writing up until the end where it got really difficult and complicated. It was then that I decided to pretend that I had always intended to improvise from this point.

Shane Meadows

Credits

Filmography

1994 (from July)
Where's the Money, Ronnie? (10 min)
Where's the Money, Ronnie? 2 (15 min)
The Datsun Connection (13 min)
The Murderer (5 min)
Little Man (10 min, Doc)
The Cleaner (4 min)

1995
The Pasta Twist (11 min)
The Stretch (16 min)
The Allotment Show (2 min)
Sneinton Junction (6 min)
Jock and John are Neighbours (7 min)
Black Wiggow (10 min)
King of the Gypsies (6 min Doc)
King of the Gypsies (10 min Doc)
Kill me now, Mummy (7 min)
Karate Youth (3 min)
The Zombie Squad (11 min)
Where's The Money Ronnie? 3 (14 min)
A Glyde in the Park (5 mins)

1996
The Rise and Fall of a Protection Agency (20 min)
Where's the Money Ronnie? 4 (10 min)
Simon Stanway is Not Dead (18 min)
Smalltime (60 min)
Torino Torino (15 min Doc)
The Church of Alan Darcy (8 min)

1997
TwentyFourSeven (94 min)
Come Back Dominic Dillon (12 min)
Waiting for the Winter (16 min)
In the Meantime Afternoon (20 min Doc)
A Room for Romeo Brass (13 min)

1998
Paul, Simon, Dominic and Snowy Cabrerra (14 min)
Daihatsu Domino (9 mins)